Masterpieces of

Velazquez

(1907)

ISBN-13 : 978-1512309034

ISBN-10 : 1512309036

Notice

This documentary study use historic, archived documents.

Because of this, some pages may look blurry or low quality.

Still are included in this book because they have

high value from critical, documentary, historical,

informative and journalistic point of view .

Dtp
and
visual art

Iacob Adrian

THE
MASTERPIECES
OF
VELAZQUEZ

Sixty reproductions of photographs from the original paintings, principally by F. Hanfstaengl, affording examples of the different characteristics of the Artist's work

Author statement

This is a series of art books .

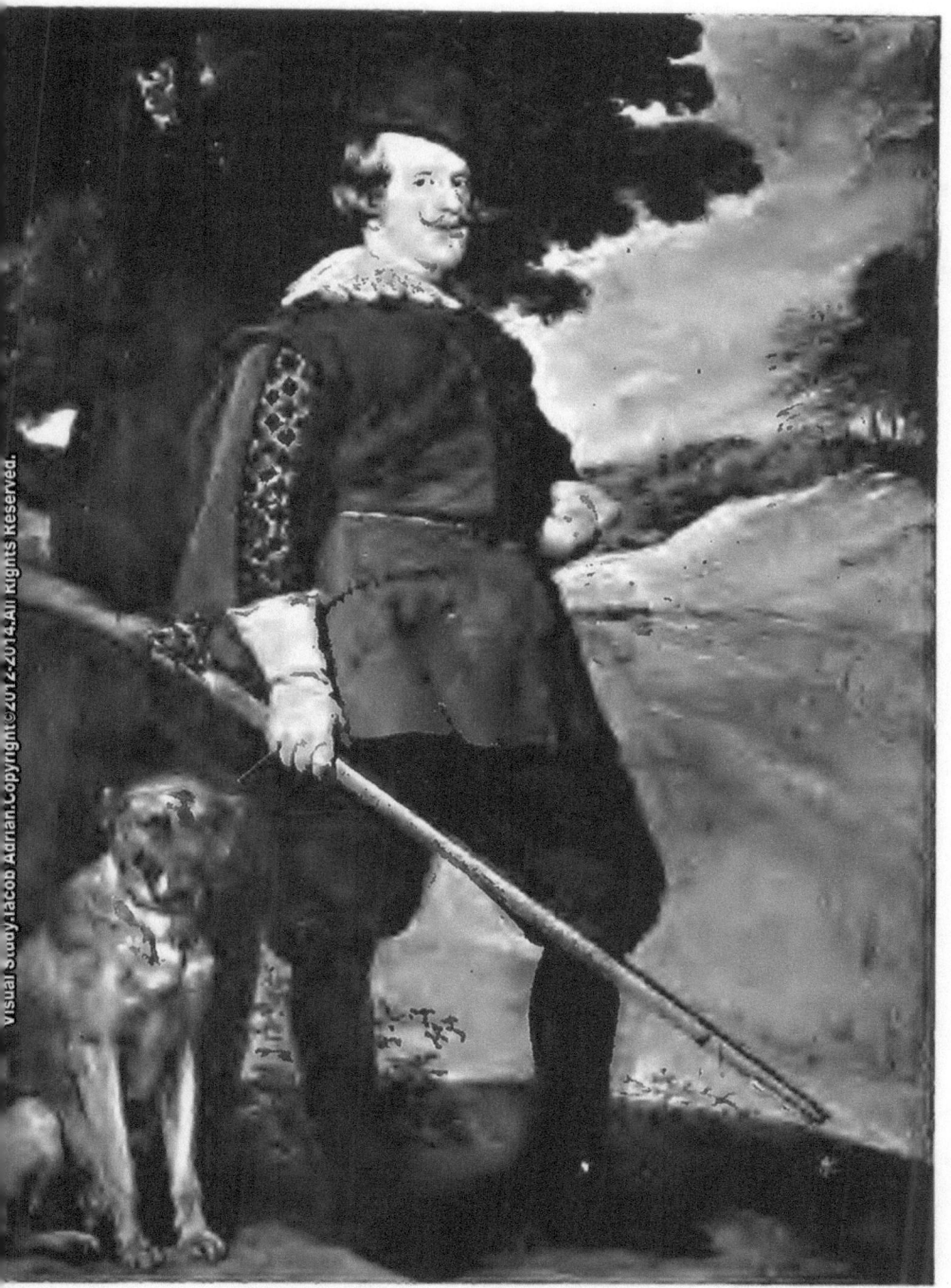

PHILIP IV.
(*Prado, Madrid*)

PHILIPPE IV.
(*Prado, Madrid*)

PHILIPP IV.
(*Madrid, Prado*)
D. Anderson, Photo.

This little Book conveys the greetings of

....

to

....

_____

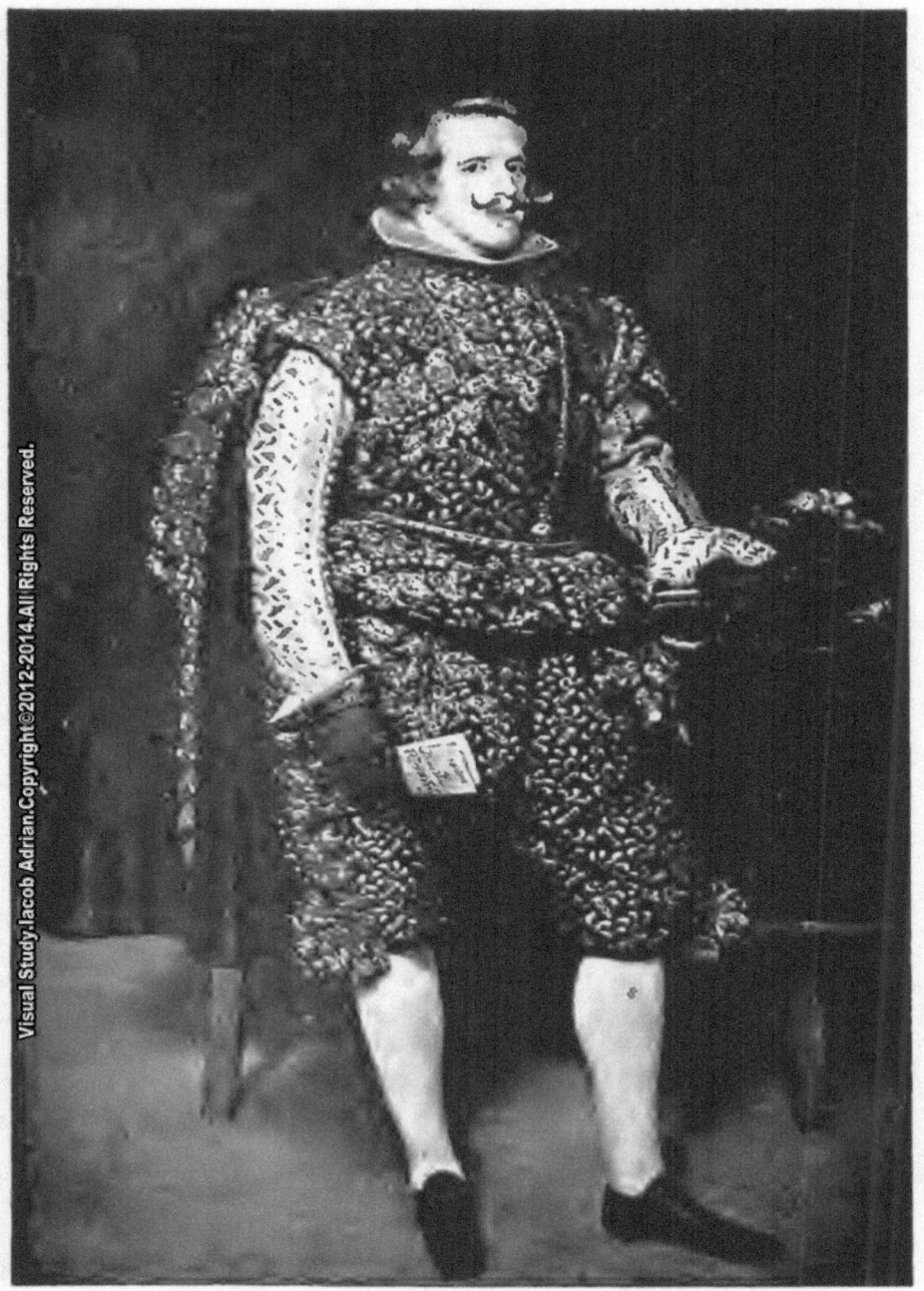

PHILIP IV.   PHILIPPE IV.
(*National Gallery, London*) (*Galerie nationale, Londres*)
PHILIPP IV.
(*London, Nationalgalerie*)
F. Hanfstaengl, Photo.

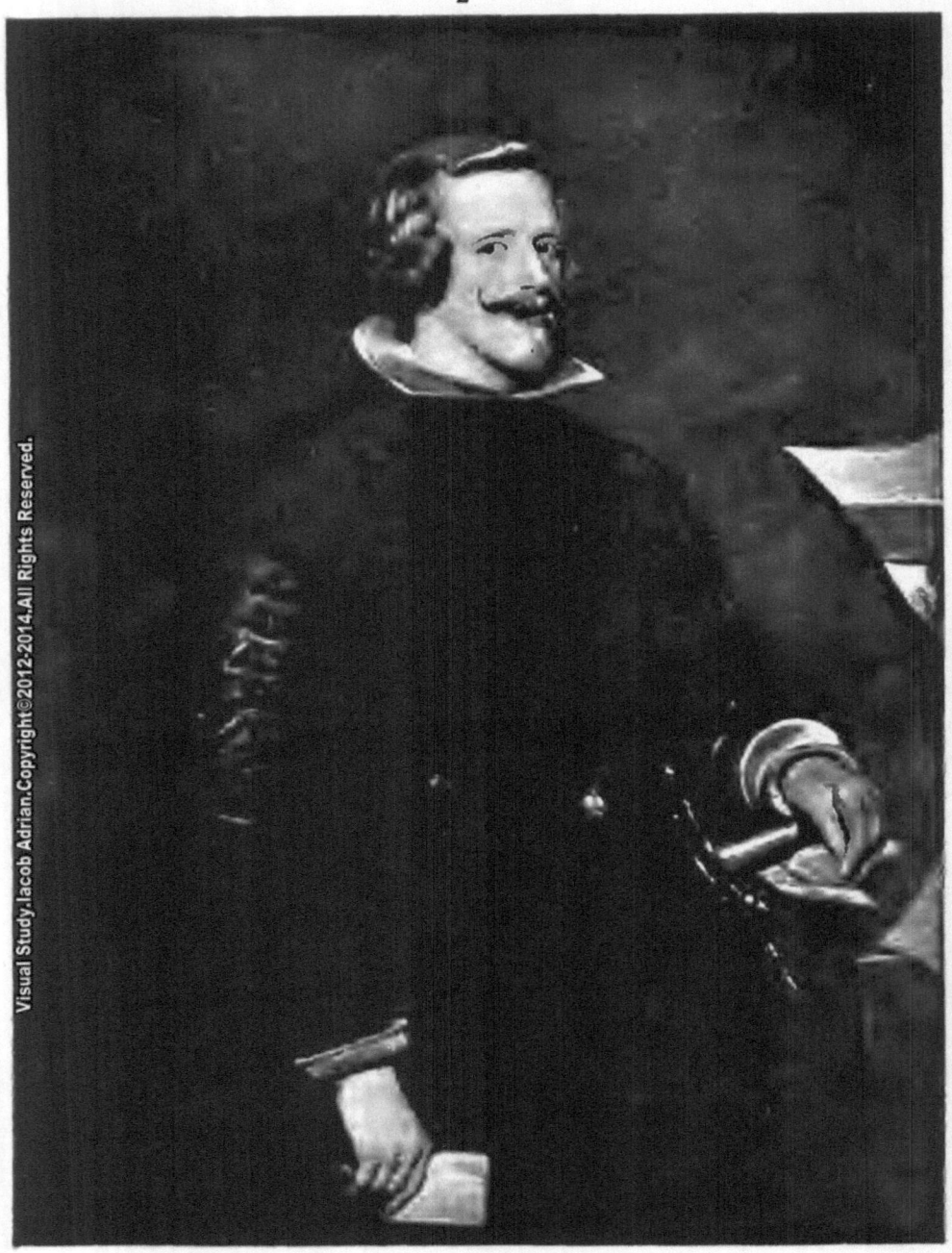

PHILIP IV.   PHILIPPE IV.
(*Imperial Gallery, Vienna*)   (*Galerie impériale, Vienne*)
PHILIPP IV.
(*Wien, Kaiserl. Galerie*)
F. Hanfstaengl, Photo.

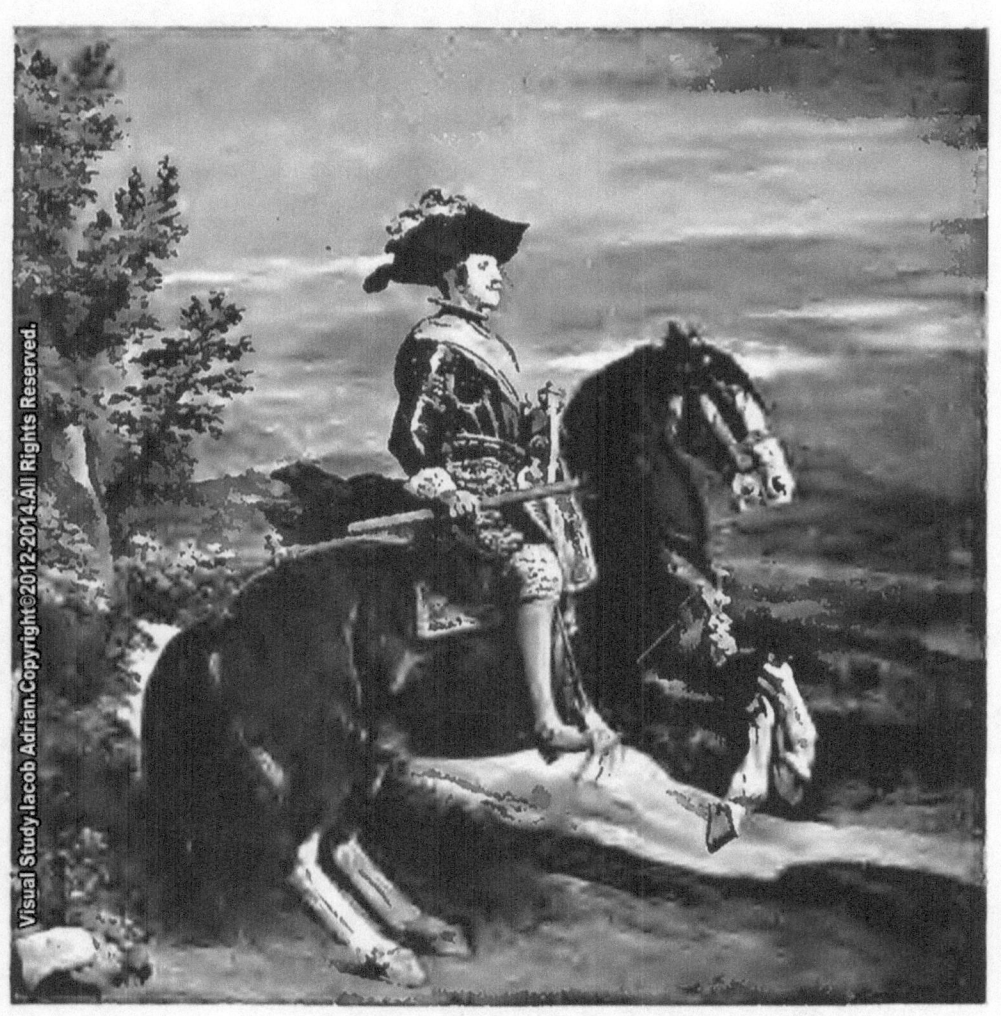

PHILIP IV.
(*Prado, Madrid*)

PHILIPPE IV.
(*Prado, Madrid*)

PHILIPP IV.
(*Madrid, Prado*)
D. Anderson, Photo.

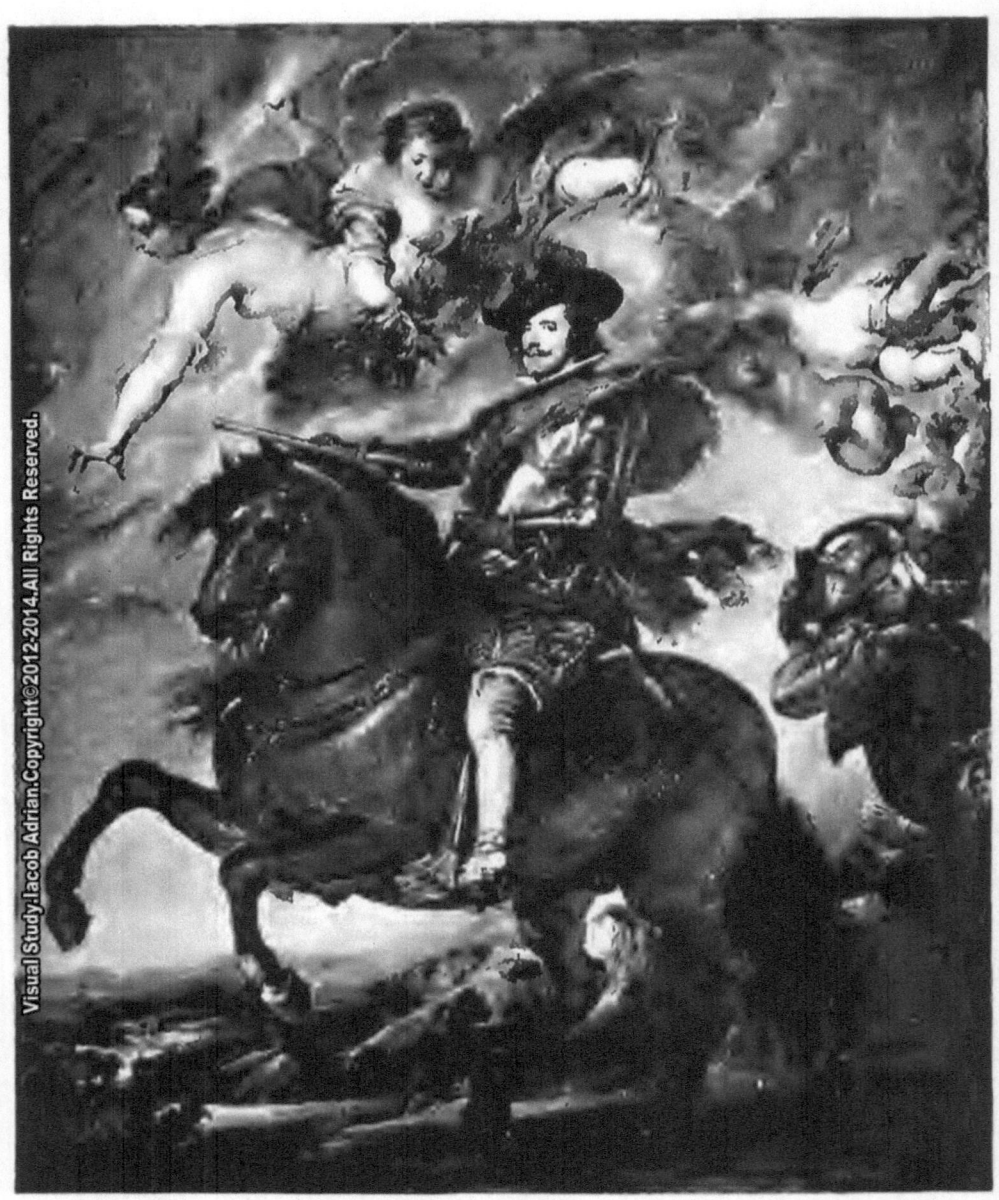

PHILIP IV.
(*Uffizi, Florence*)

PHILIPPE IV.
(*Galerie des Uffizi, Florence*)

PHILIPP IV.
(*Florenz, Uffizien*)
F. Hanfstaengl, Photo.

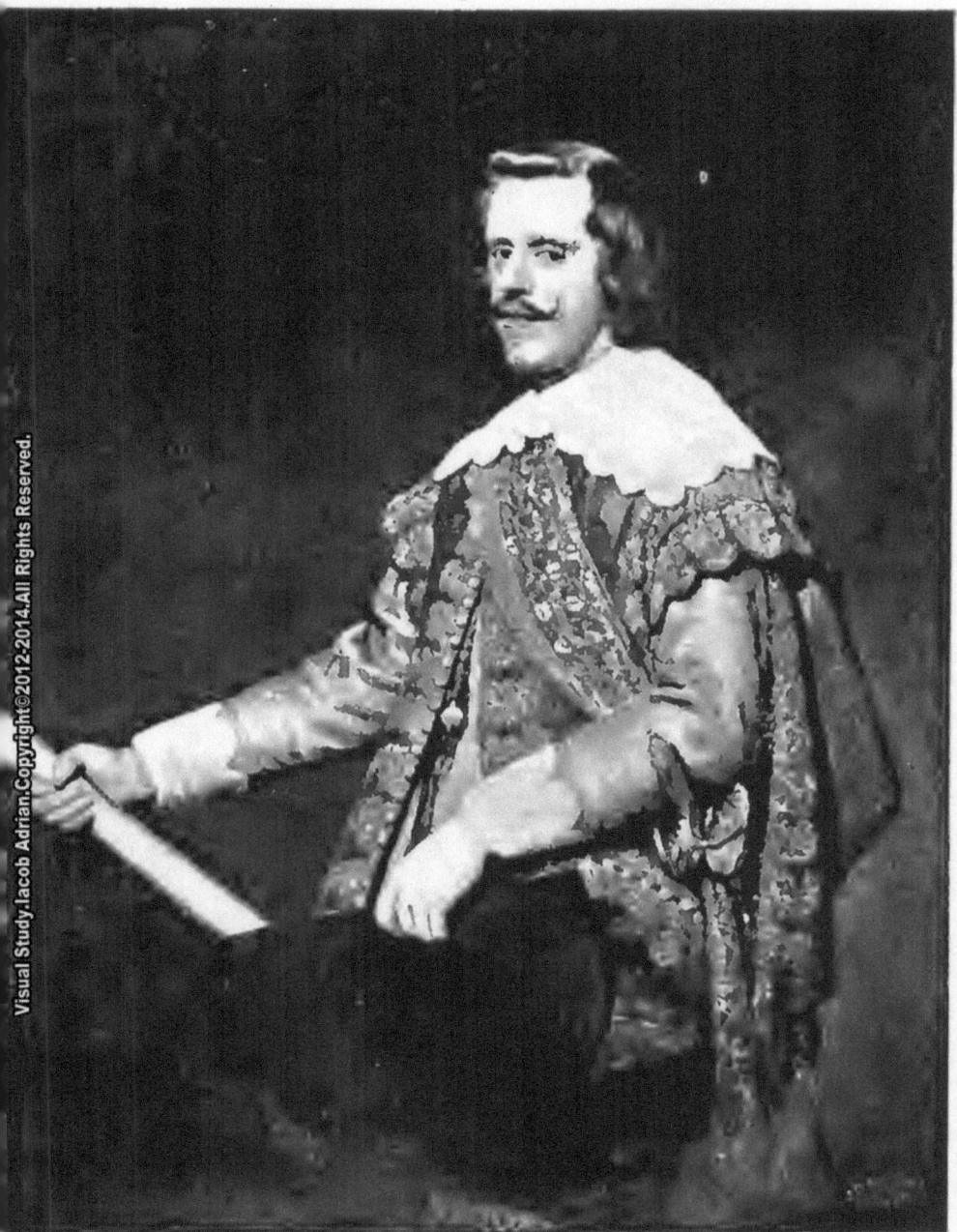

PHILIP IV.
(*Dulwich Gallery*)

PHILIPPE IV.
(*Galerie, Dulwich*)

PHILIPP IV.
(*Dulwich, Galerie*)
F. Hanfstaengl, Photo.

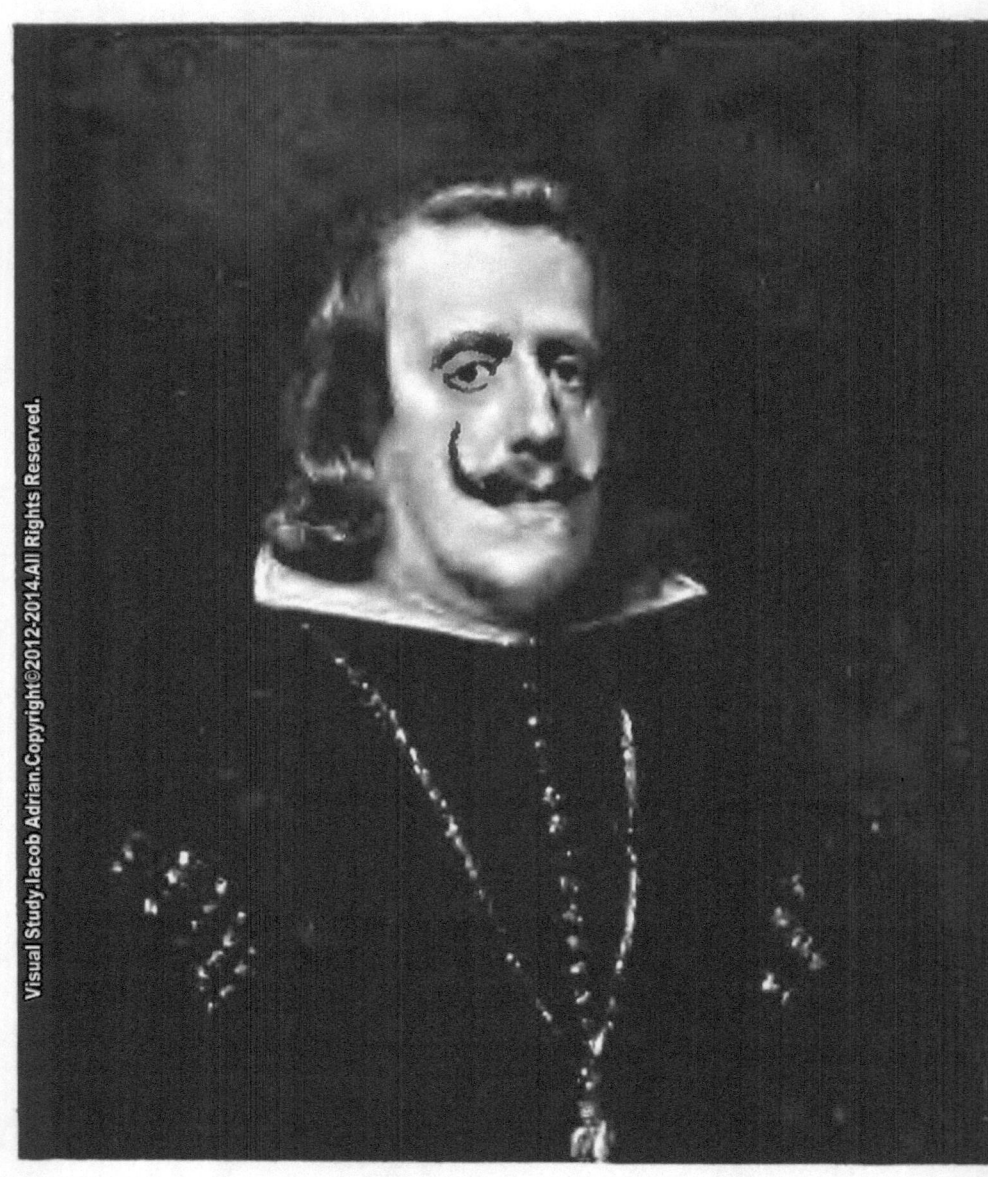

PHILIP IV.
(*National Gallery, London*)

PHILIPPE IV.
(*Galerie nationale, Londres*)

PHILIPP IV.
(*London, Nationalgalerie*)
F. Hanfstaengl, Photo.

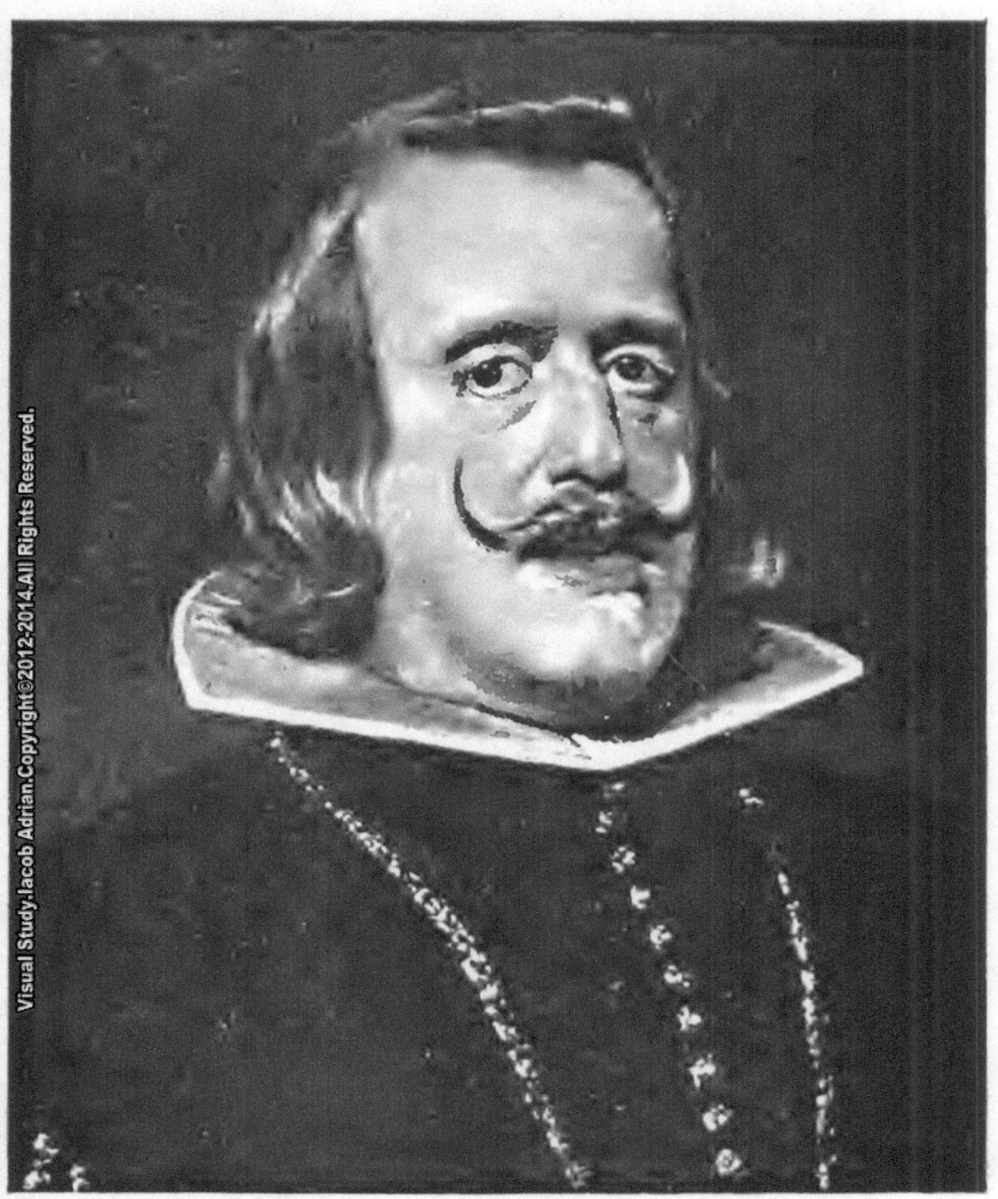

PHILIP IV.   PHILIPPE IV.
(*Imperial Gallery, Vienna*)   (*Galerie impériale, Vienne*)
PHILIPP IV.
(*Wien, Kaiserl. Galerie*)
F. Hanfstaengl, Photo.

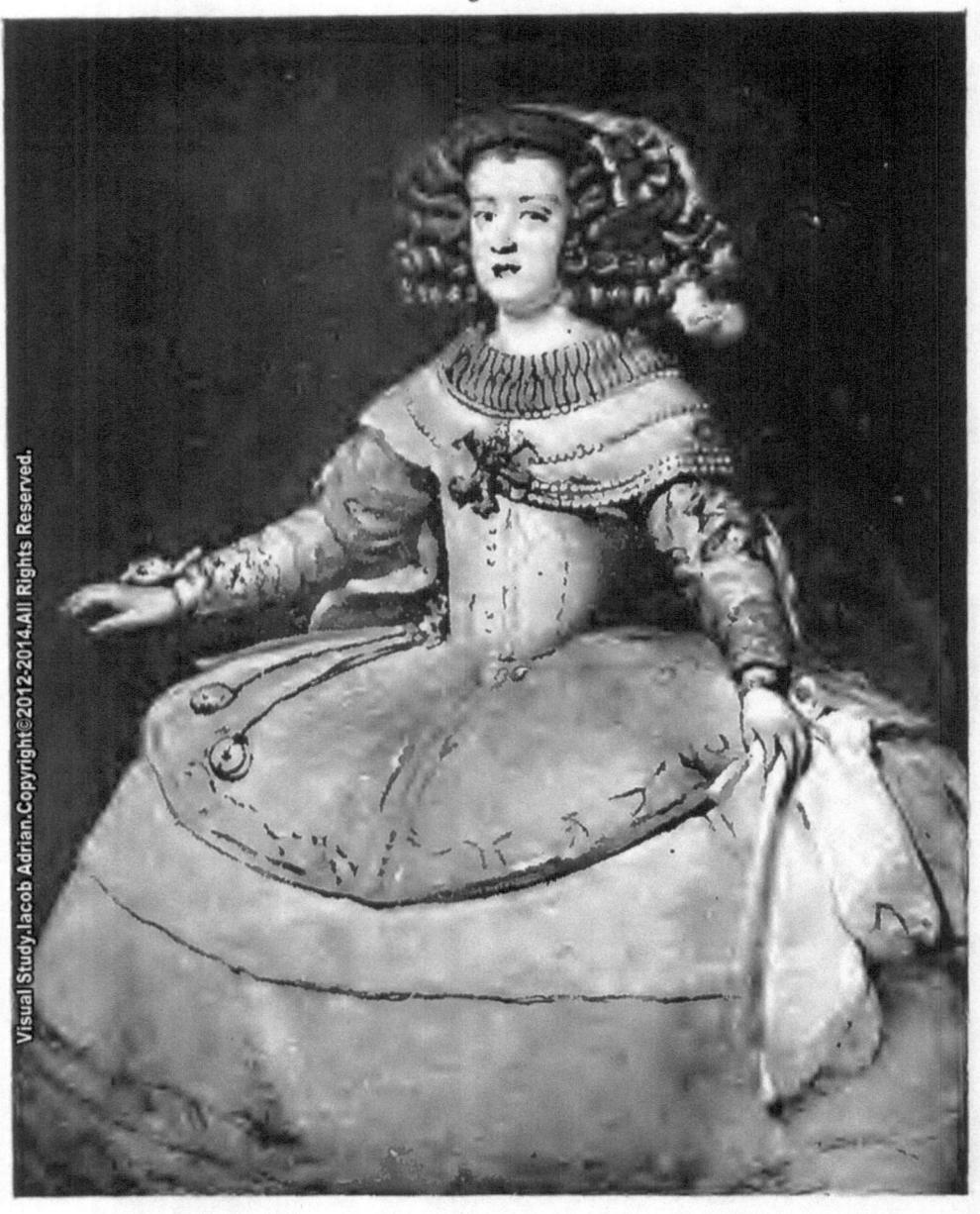

QUEEN MARIANA OF AUSTRIA,   LA REINE MARIE-ANNE D'AUTRICHE
SECOND WIFE OF PHILIP IV.   SECONDE FEMME DE PHILIPPE IV.
(*Imperial Gallery, Vienna*)   (*Galerie impériale, Vienne*)
KÖNIGIN MARIANNE VON ÖSTERREICH, ZWEITE GEMAHLIN
PHILIPPS IV.
(*Wien, Kaiserl. Galerie*)
F. Hanfstaengl, Photo.

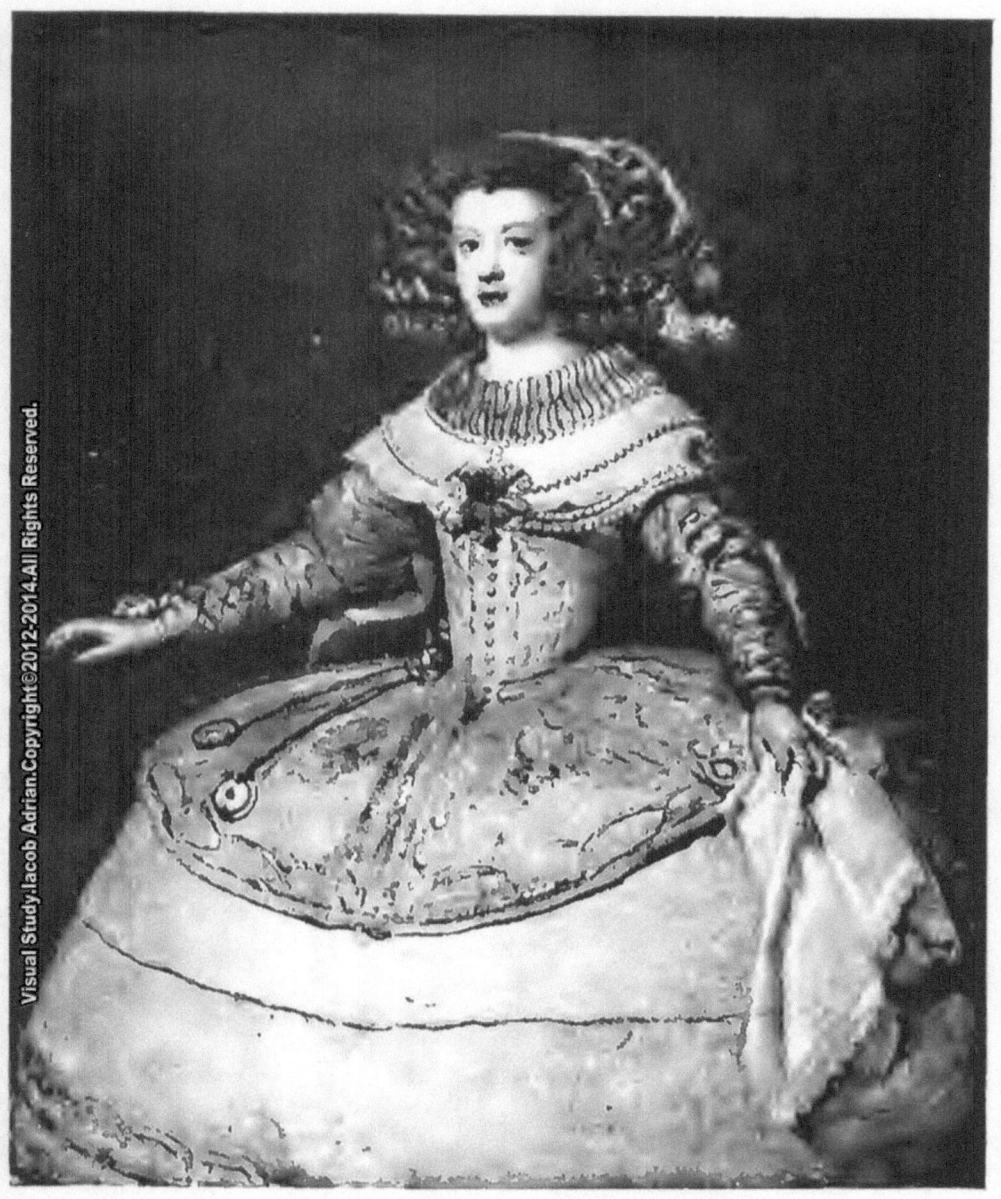

QUEEN MARIANA OF AUSTRIA   LA REINE MARIE-ANNE D'AUTRICHE
(Imperial Gallery, Vienna)   (Galerie impériale, Vienne)
KÖNIGIN MARIANNE VON ÖSTERREICH
(Wien, Kaiserl. Galerie)
F. Hanfstaengl, Photo.

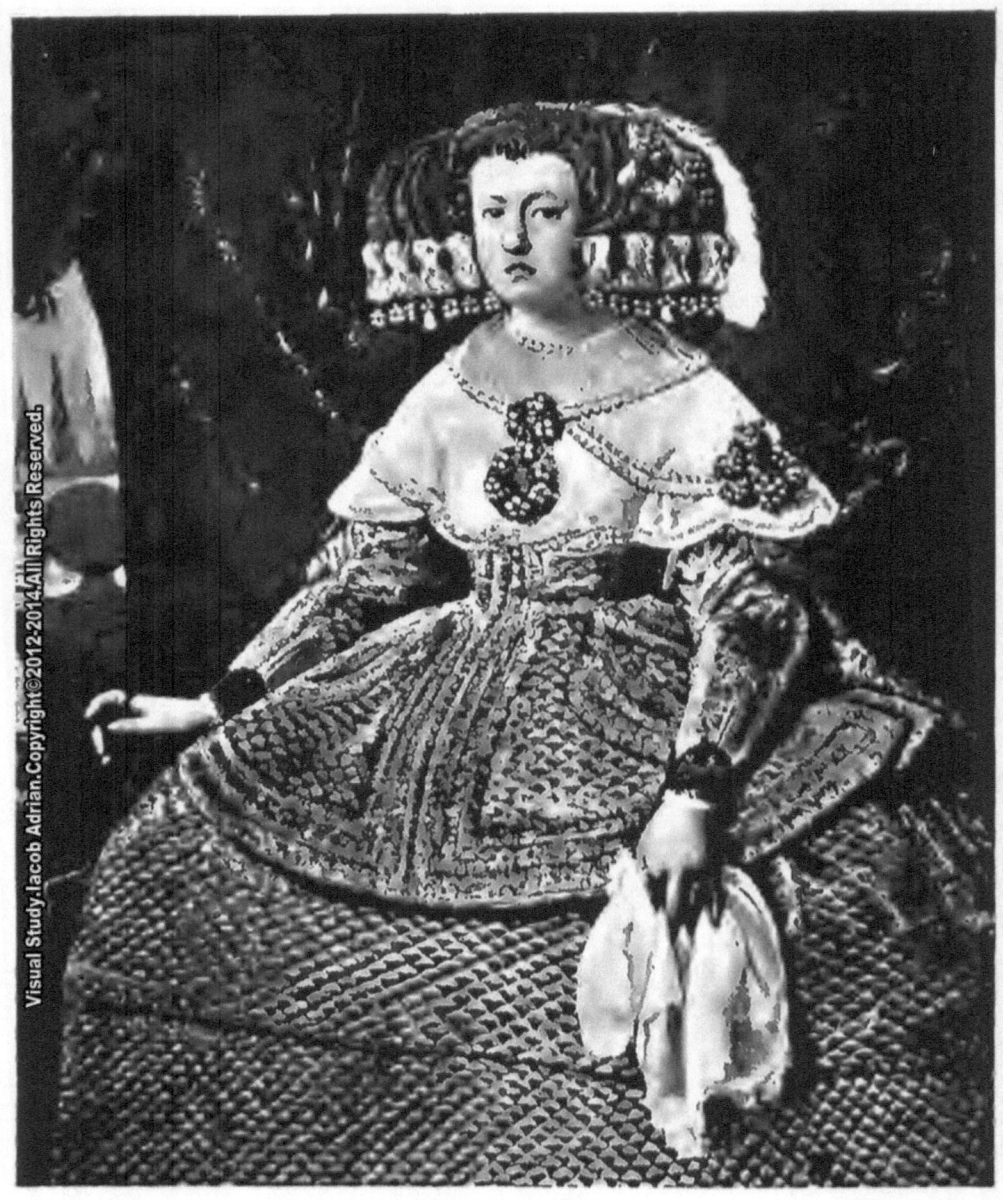

QUEEN MARIANA OF AUSTRIA   LA REINE MARIE-ANNE D'AUTRICHE
(*Imperial Gallery, Vienna*)   (*Galerie impériale, Vienne*)
KÖNIGIN MARIANNE VON ÖSTERREICH
(*Wien, Kaiserl. Galerie*)
F. Hanfstaengl, Photo.

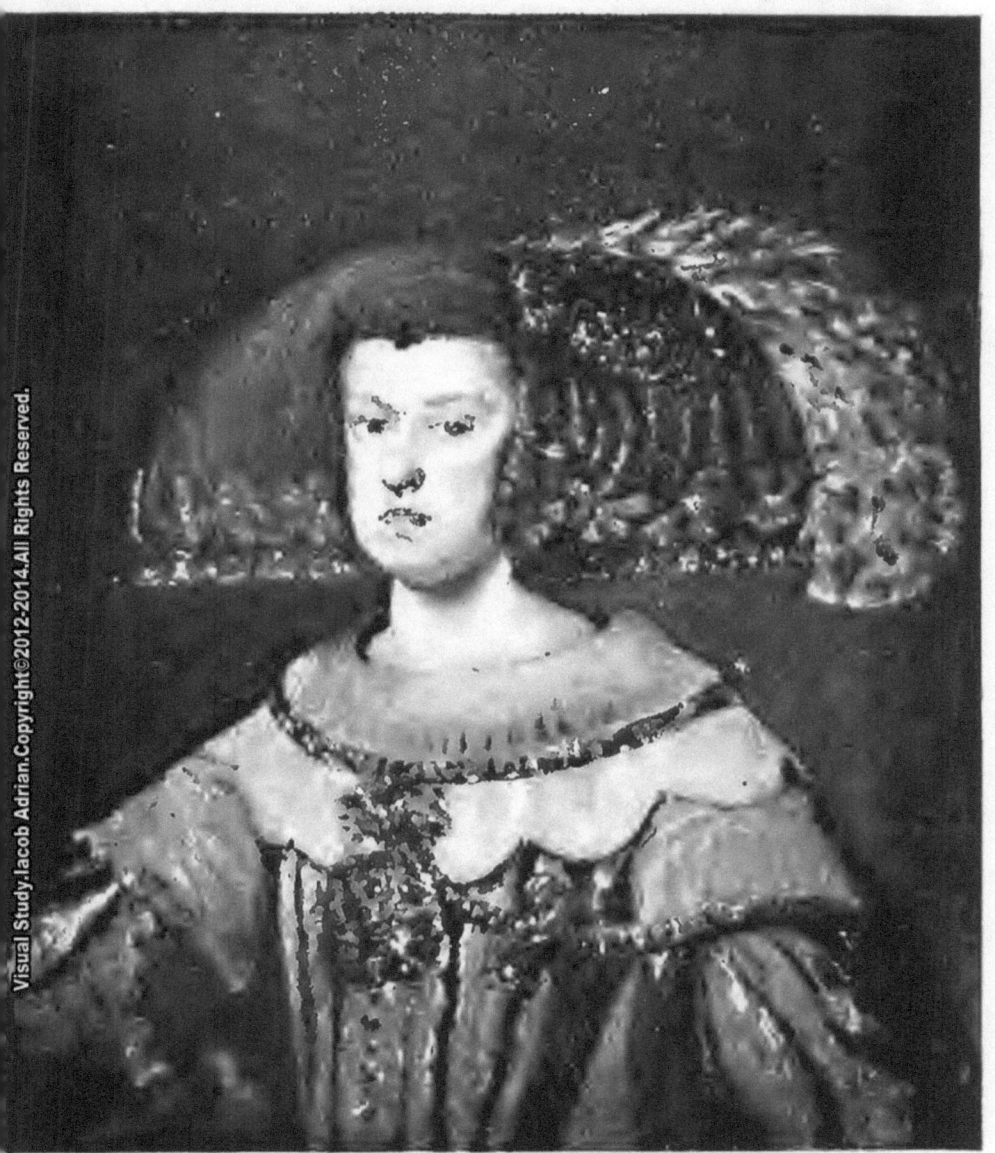

QUEEN MARIANA OF AUSTRIA   LA REINE MARIE-ANNE D'AUTRICHE
(*Brabazon Collection, London*)   (*Collection Brabazon, Londres*)
KÖNIGIN MARIANNE VON ÖSTERREICH
(*London, Sammlung Brabazon*)
F. Hanfstaengl, Photo.

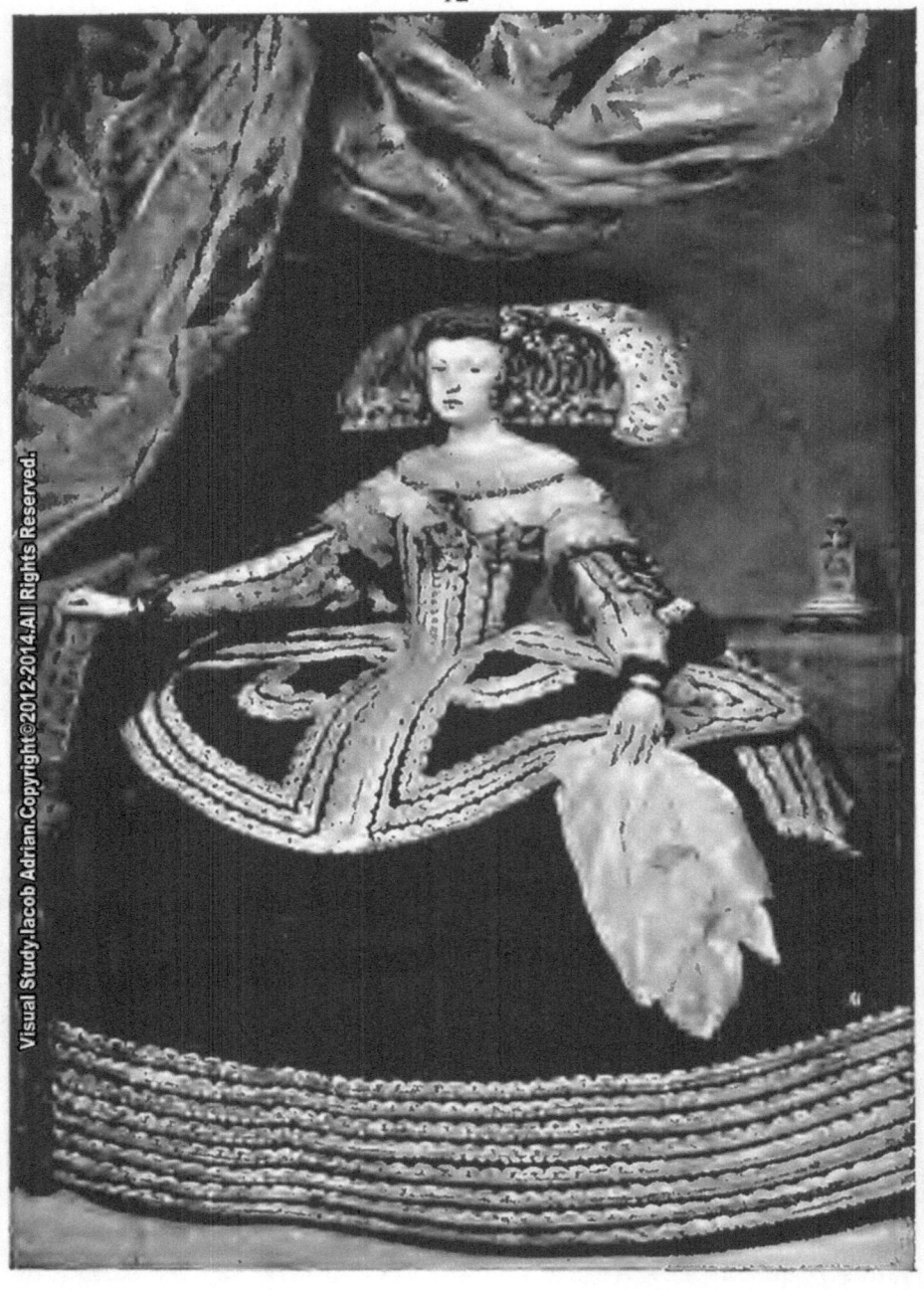

QUEEN MARIANA OF   LA REINE MARIE-ANNE
AUSTRIA   D'AUTRICHE
(*Prado, Madrid*)   (*Prado, Madrid*)
KÖNIGIN MARIANNE VON ÖSTERREICH
(*Madrid, Prado*)
D. Anderson, Photo.

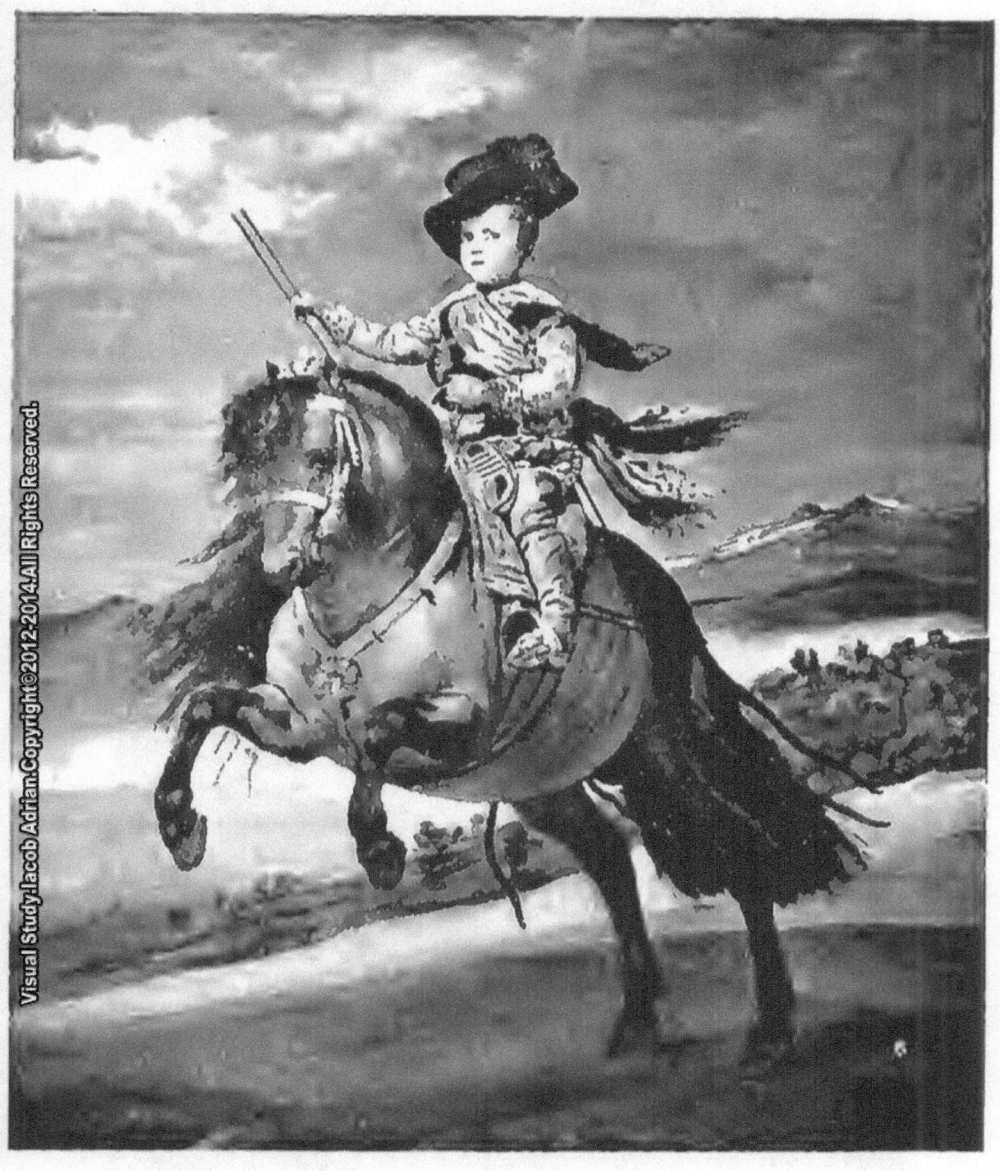

PRINCE BALTHASAR CARLOS,   LE PRINCE BALTHAZAR-CHARLES,
SON OF PHILIP IV.   FILS DE PHILIPPE IV.
(*Prado, Madrid*)   (*Prado, Madrid*)
INFANT BALTHASAR CARLOS, SOHN PHILIPPS IV.
(*Madrid, Prado*)
D. Anderson, Photo.

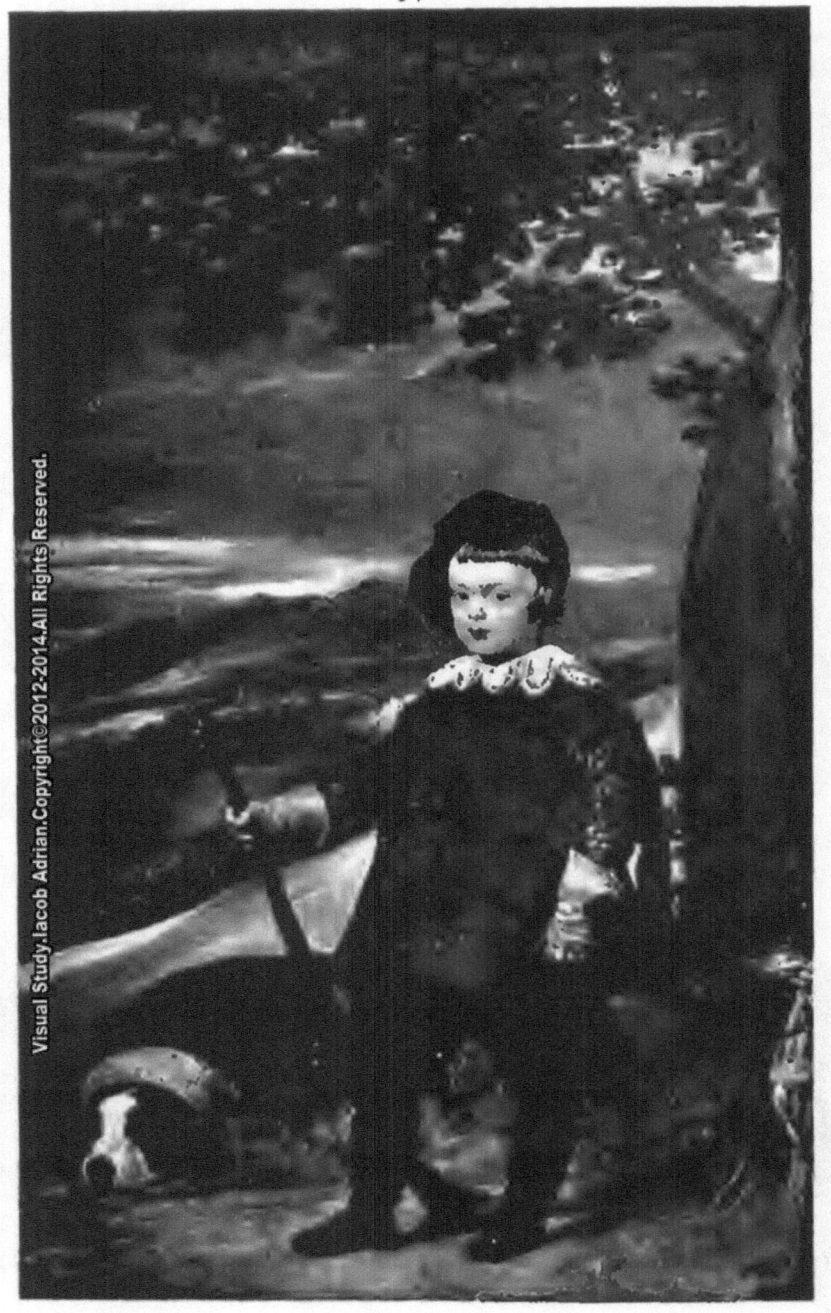

PRINCE BALTHASAR CARLOS   LE PRINCE BALTHAZAR-CHARLES
(Prado, Madrid)   (Prado, Madrid)
INFANT BALTHASAR CARLOS
(Madrid, Prado)
D. Anderson, Photo.

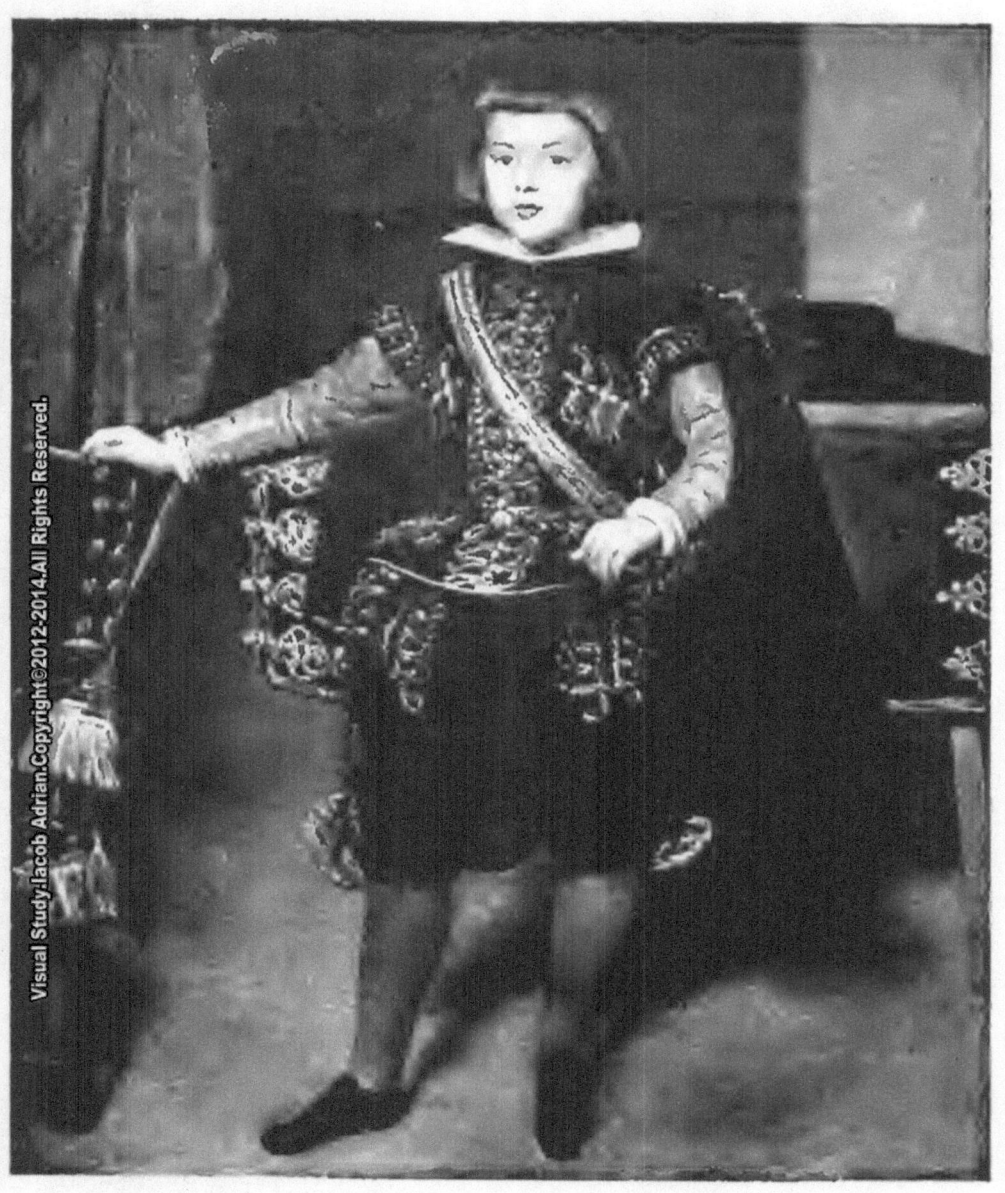

PRINCE BALTHASAR CARLOS   LE PRINCE BALTHAZAR-CHARLES
(*Imperial Gallery, Vienna*)   (*Galerie impériale, Vienne*)
INFANT BALTHASAR CARLOS
(*Wien, Kaiserl. Galerie*)
F. Hanfstaengl, Photo.

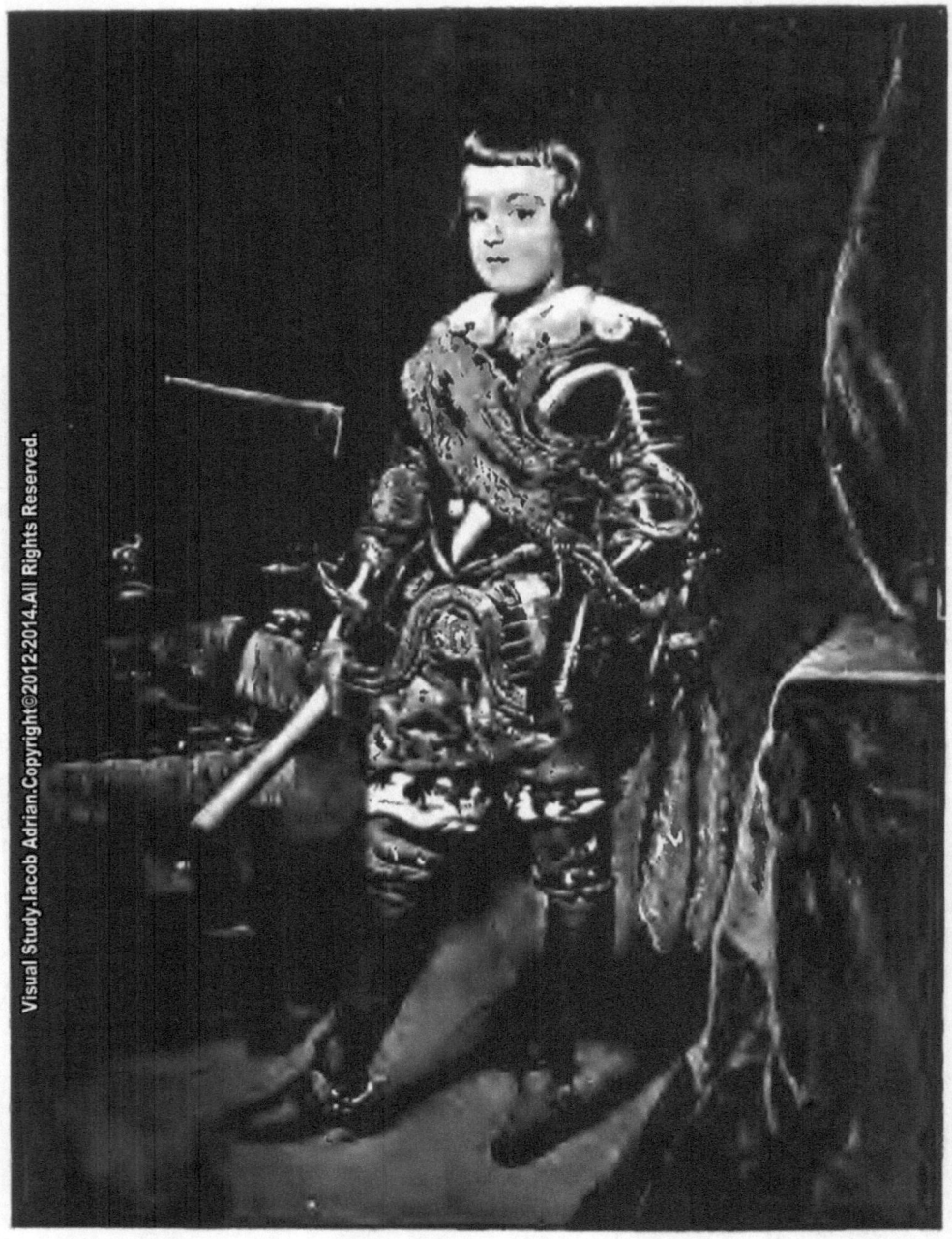

PRINCE BALTHASAR CARLOS   LE PRINCE BALTHAZAR-CHARLES
(Royal Gallery, The Hague)   *(Musée royal, La Haye)*
INFANT BALTHASAR CARLOS
(Haag, Kgl. Galerie)
F. Hanfstaengl, Photo.

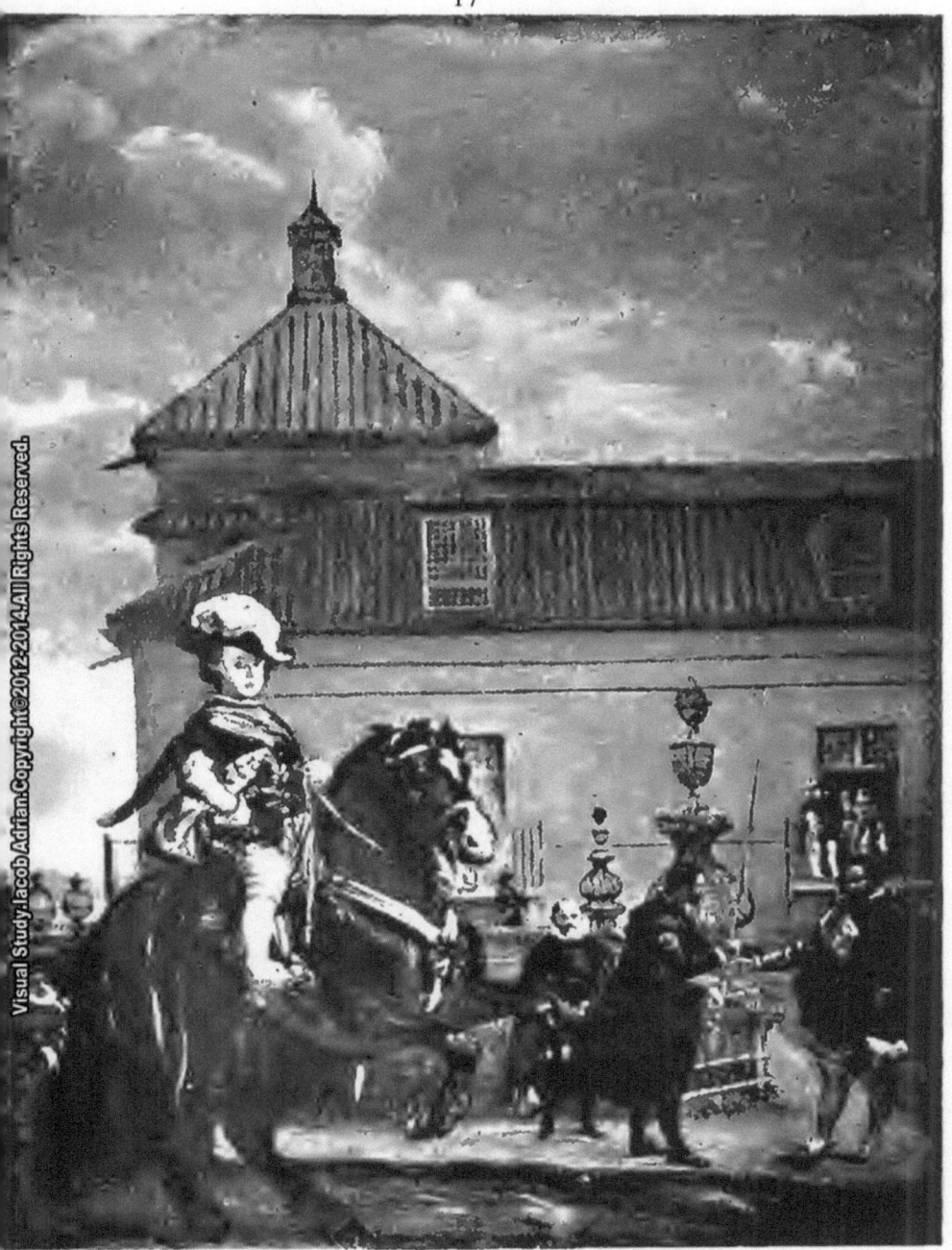

PRINCE BALTHASAR CARLOS   LE PRINCE BALTHAZAR-CHARLES
(*Duke of Westminster, London*)   (*Duc de Westminster, Londres*)
INFANT BALTHASAR CARLOS
(*Herzog von Westminster, London*)
F. Hanfstaengl, Photo.

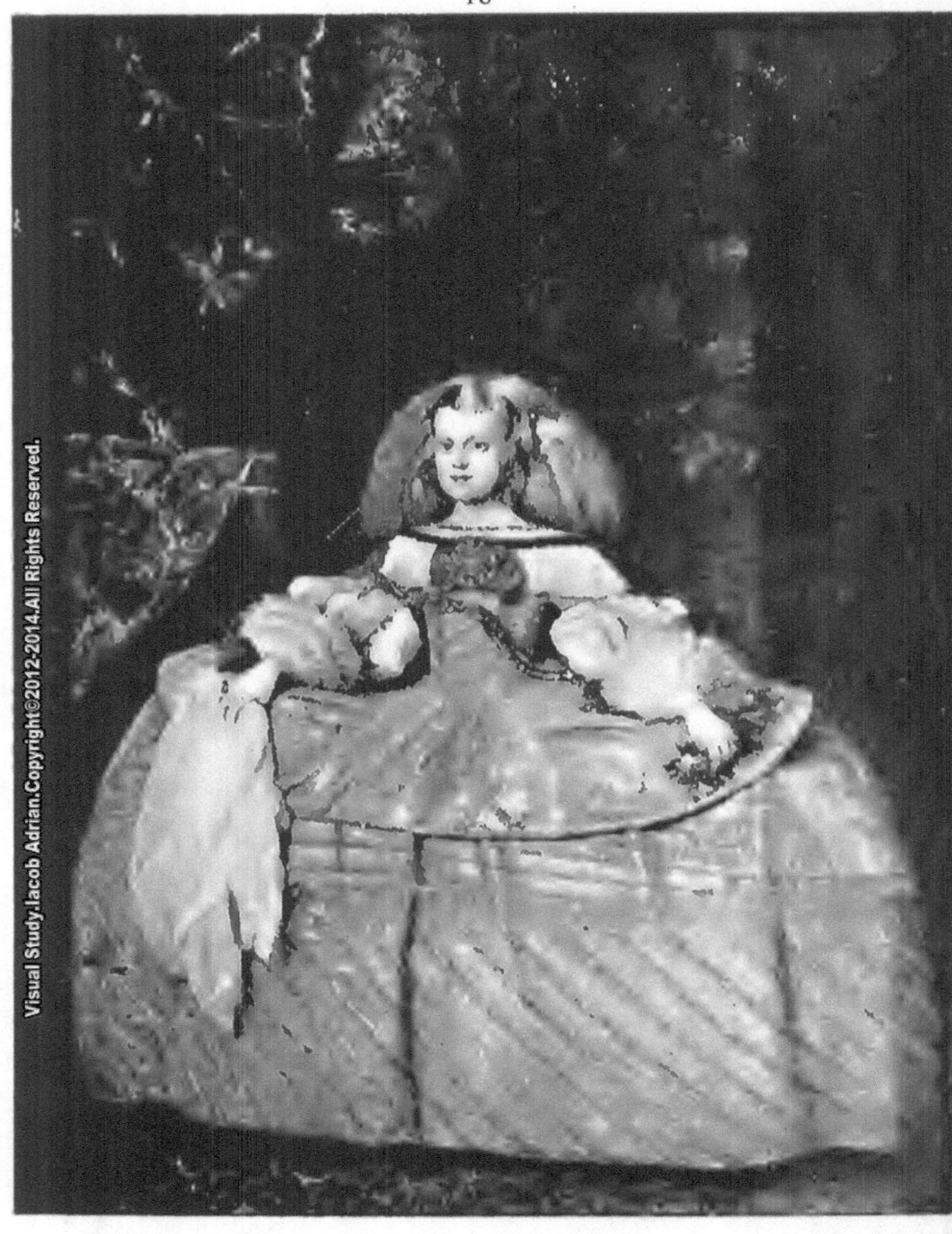

PRINCESS MARGARET,   LA PRINCESSE MARGUERITE,
DAUGHTER OF PHILIP IV.   FILLE DE PHILIPPE IV.
(*Prado, Madrid*)   (*Prado, Madrid*)
INFANTIN MARGHERITA, TOCHTER PHILIPPS IV.
(*Madrid, Prado*)
D. Anderson, Photo.

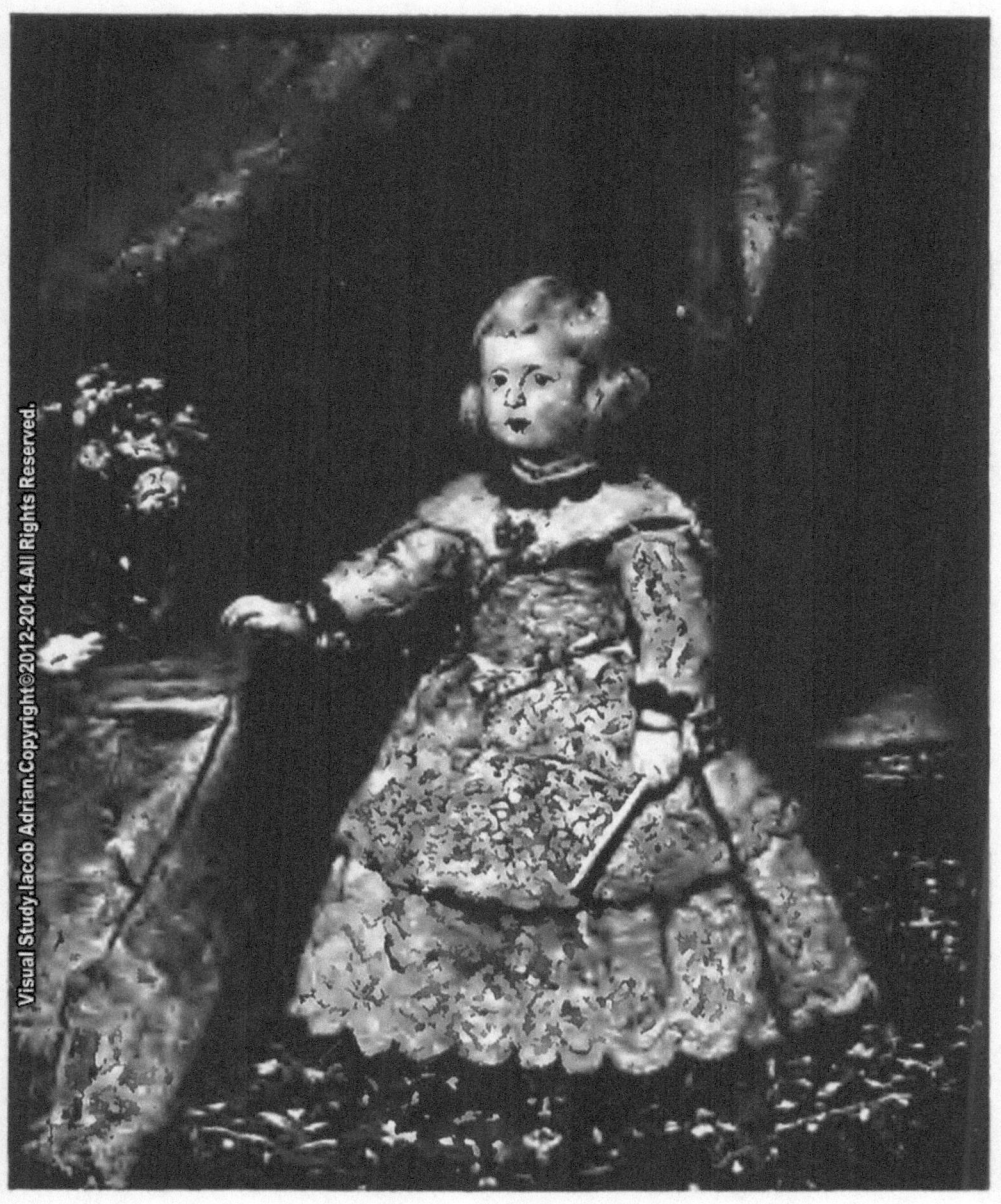

PRINCESS MARGARET   LA PRINCESSE MARGUERITE
(Imperial Gallery, Vienna)   *(Galerie impériale, Vienne)*
INFANTIN MARGHERITA
(Wien, Kaiserl. Galerie)
F. Hanfstaengl, Photo.

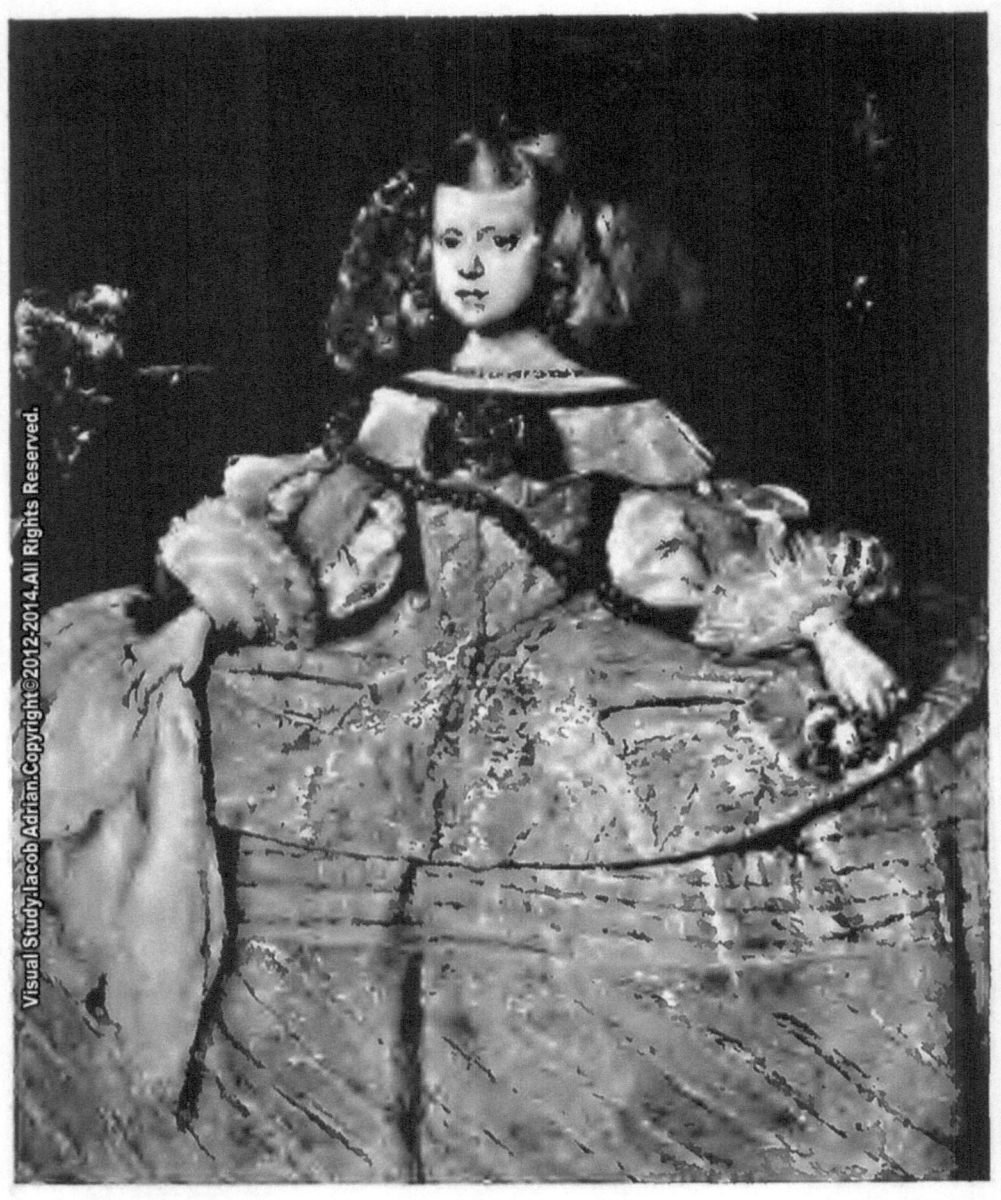

PRINCESS MARGARET   LA PRINCESSE MARGUERITE
(*Imperial Gallery, Vienna*)   (*Galerie impériale, Vienne*)
INFANTIN MARGHERITA
(*Wien, Kaiserl. Galerie*)
F. Hanfstaengl, Photo.

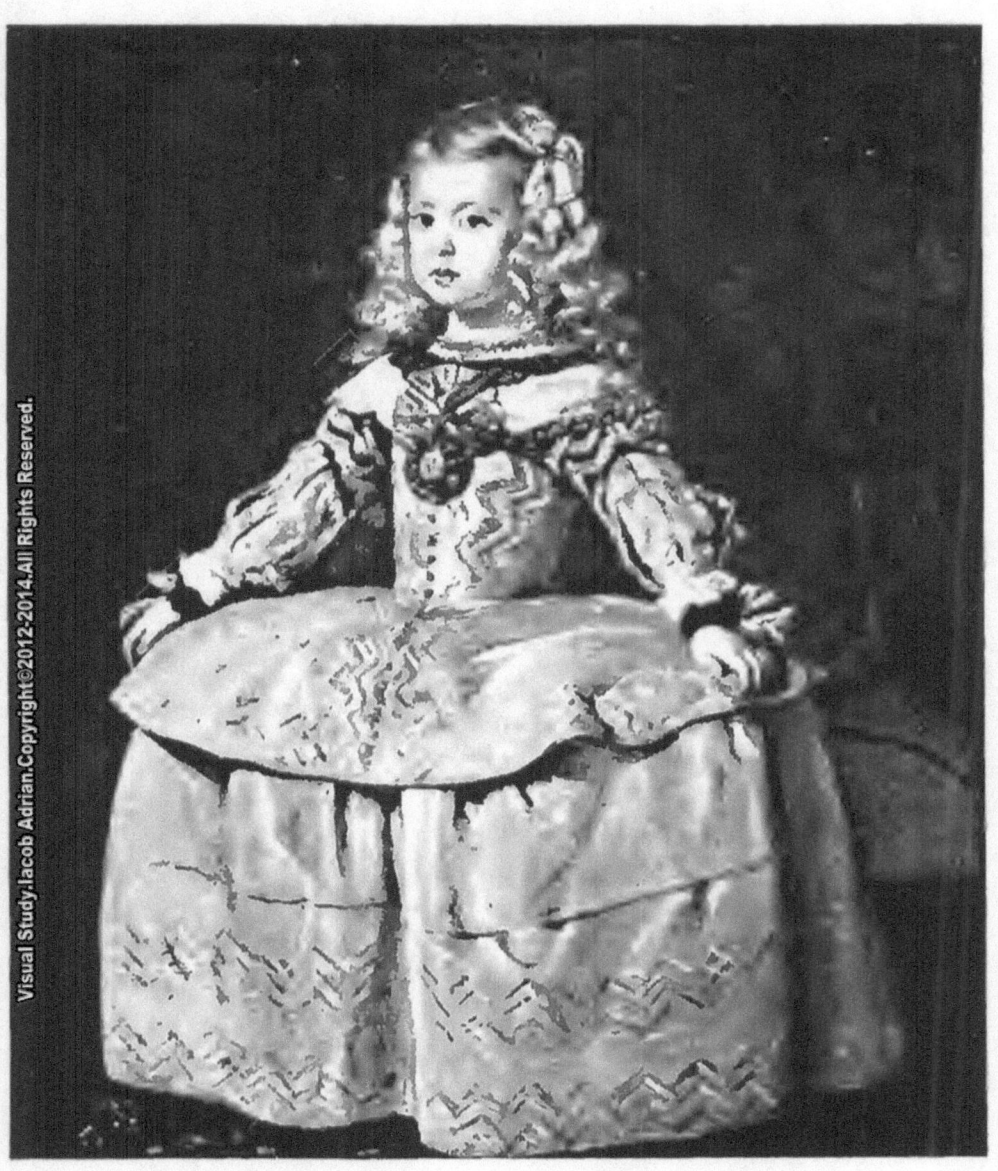

PRINCESS MARGARET   LA PRINCESSE MARGUERITE
(*Imperial Gallery, Vienna*)   (*Galerie impériale, Vienne*)
INFANTIN MARGHERITA
(*Wien, Kaiserl, Galerie*)
F. Hanfstaengl, Photo.

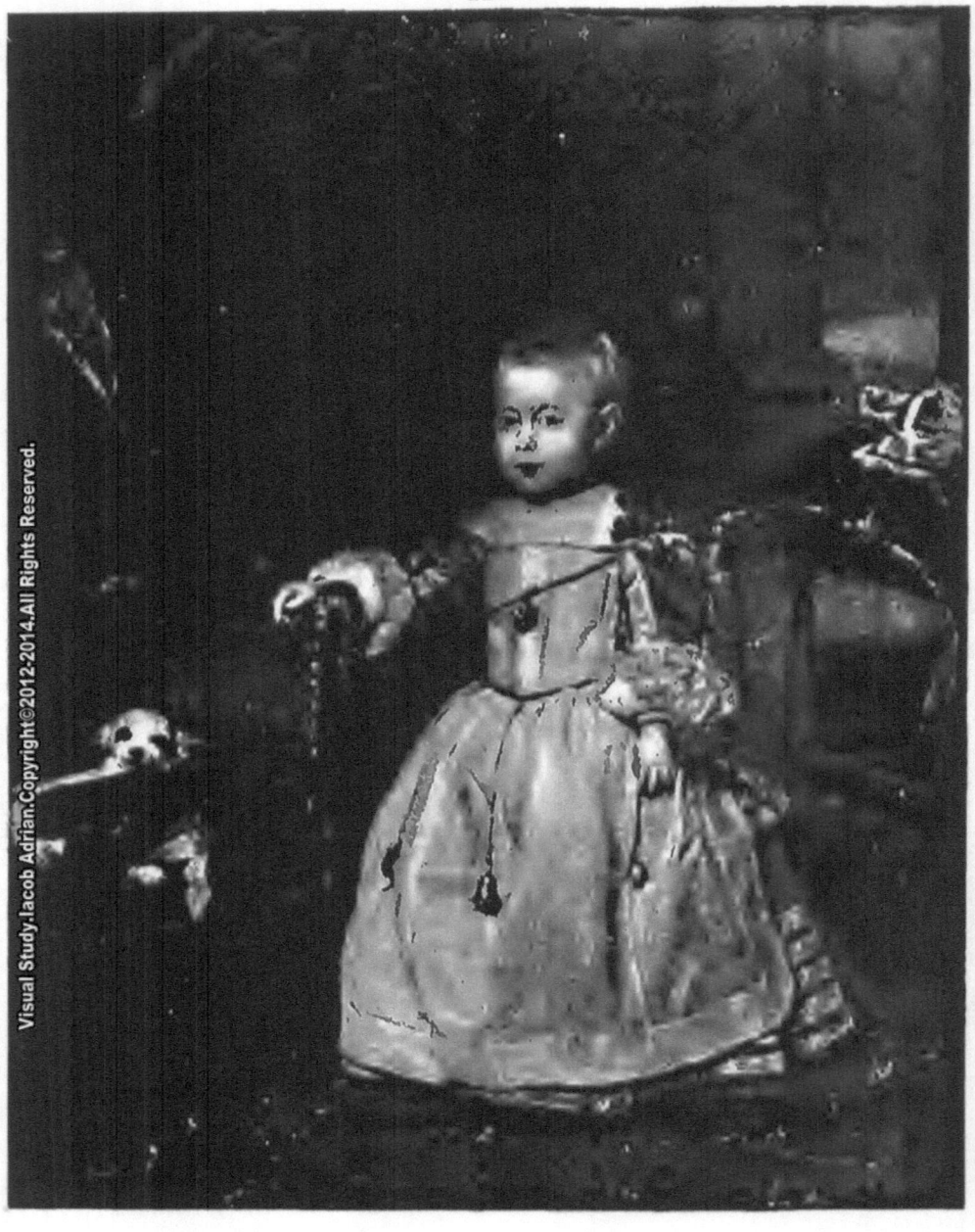

PRINCE PHILIP PROSPER,   LE PRINCE PHILIPPE PROSPER,
SON OF PHILIP IV.   FILS DE PHILIPPE IV.
(*Imperial Gallery, Vienna*)   (*Galerie impériale, Vienne*)
INFANT PHILIPP PROSPER, SOHN PHILIPPS IV.
(*Wien, Kaiserl. Galerie*)
F. Hanfstaengl, Photo.

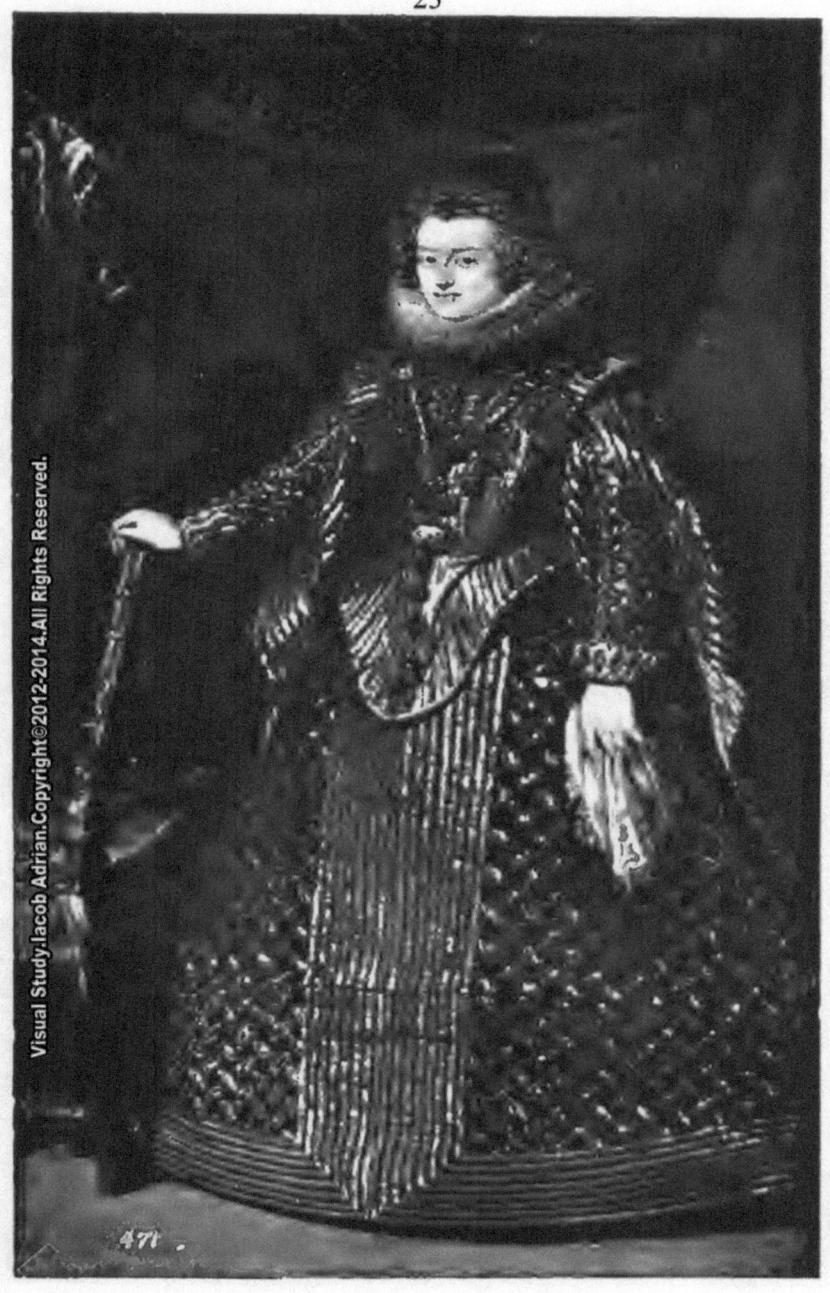

QUEEN MARY OF HUNGARY,   LA REINE MARIE DE HONGRIE,
SISTER OF PHILIP IV.   SŒUR DE PHILIPPE IV.
(*Royal Gallery, Berlin*)   (*Musée royal, Berlin*)
KÖNIGIN MARIA VON UNGARN, SCHWESTER PHILIPPS IV.
(*Berlin, Kgl. Galerie*)
F. Hanfstaengl, Photo.

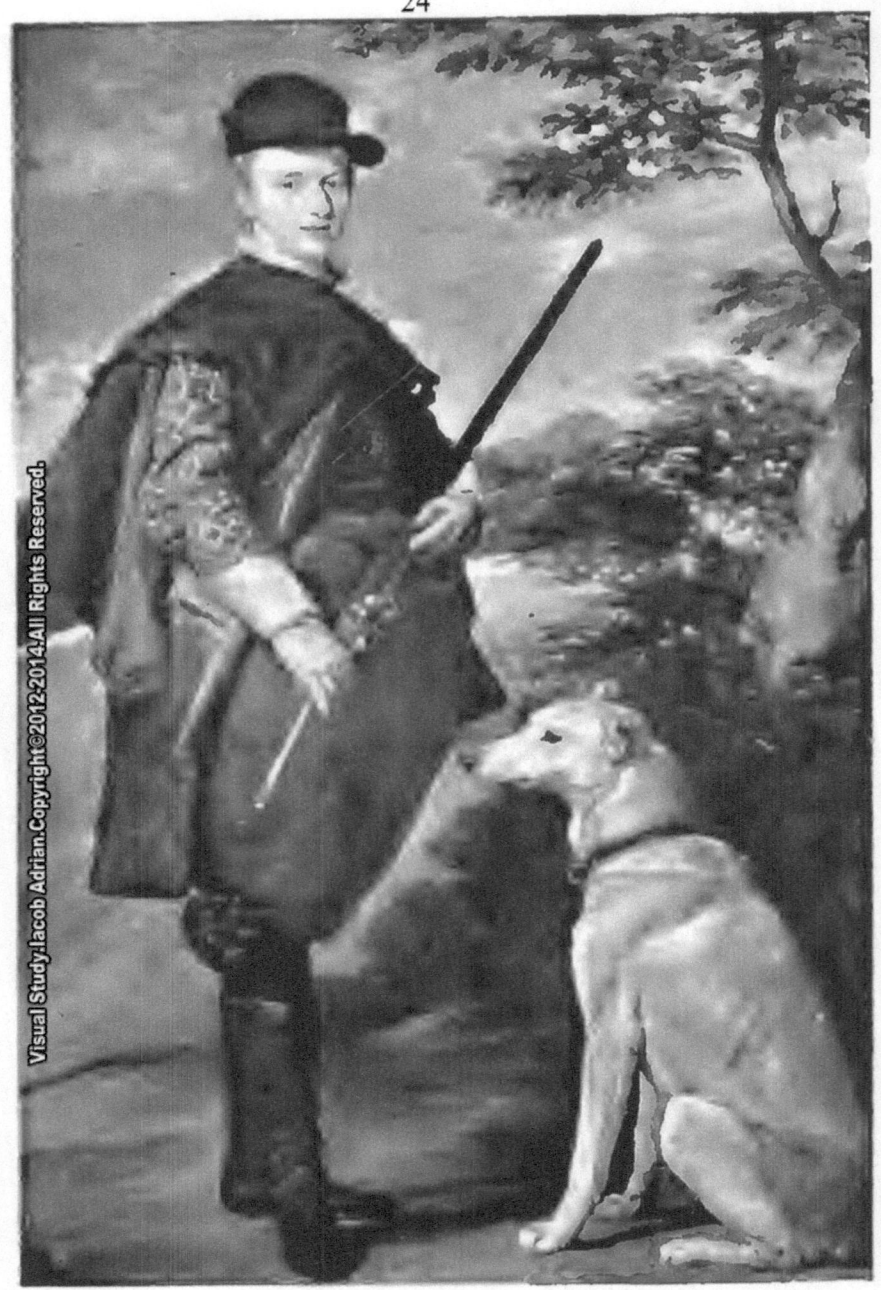

PRINCE FERDINAND,
BROTHER OF PHILIP IV.
(*Prado, Madrid*)

LE PRINCE FERDINAND,
FRÈRE DE PHILIPPE IV.
(*Prado, Madrid*)

DON FERDINAND, BRUDER PHILIPPS IV.
(*Madrid, Prado*)
D. Anderson, Photo.

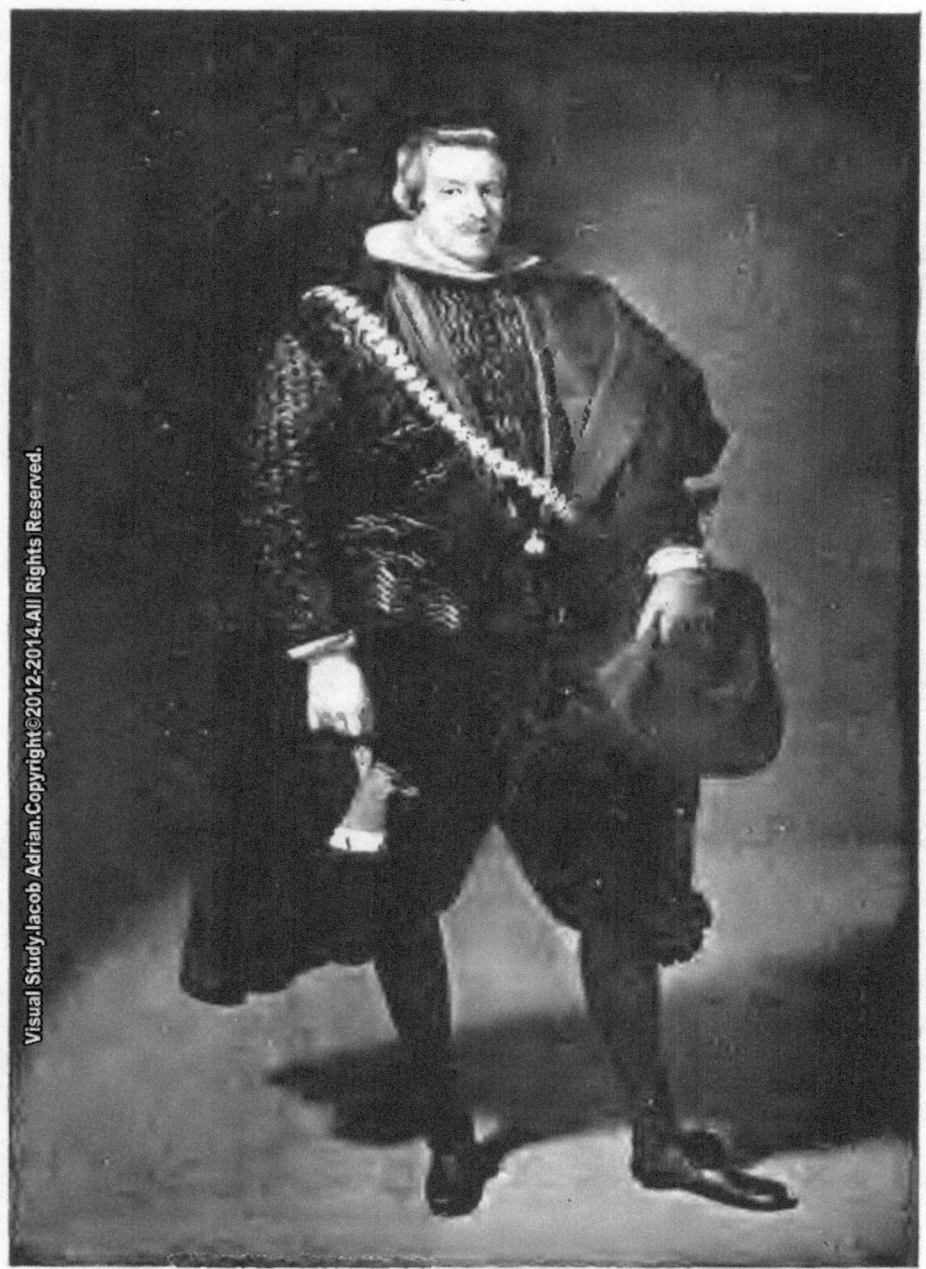

PRINCE CARLOS,
BROTHER OF PHILIP IV.
(*Prado, Madrid*)

LE PRINCE CHARLES,
FRÈRE DE PHILIPPE IV.
(*Prado, Madrid*)

DON CARLOS, BRUDER PHILIPPS IV.
(*Madrid, Prado*)
D. Anderson, Photo.

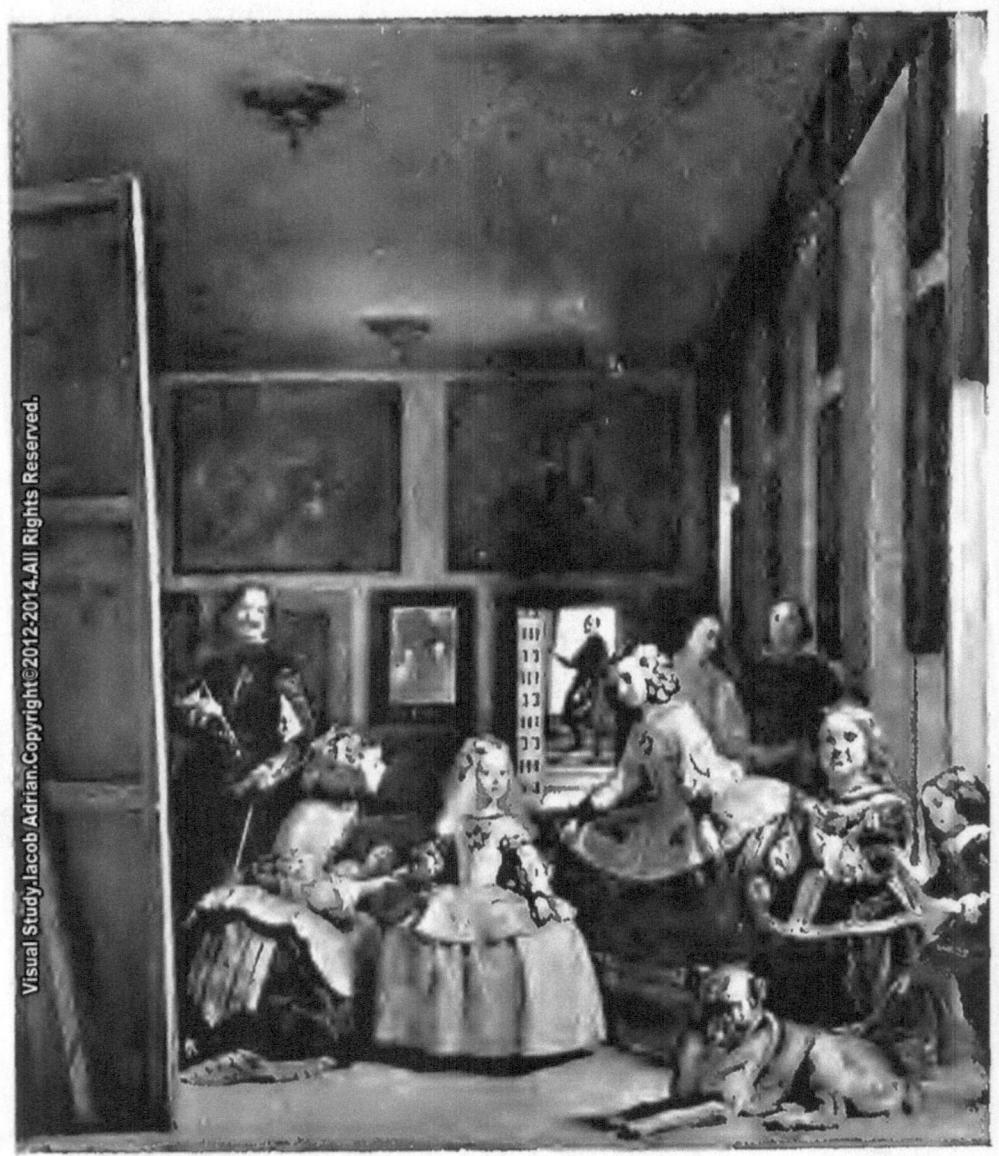

THE MAIDS OF HONOUR
(*Prado, Madrid*)

LES DAMES D'HONNEUR
(*Prado, Madrid*)

DIE HOFDAMEN
(*Madrid, Prado*)

D. Anderson, Photo.

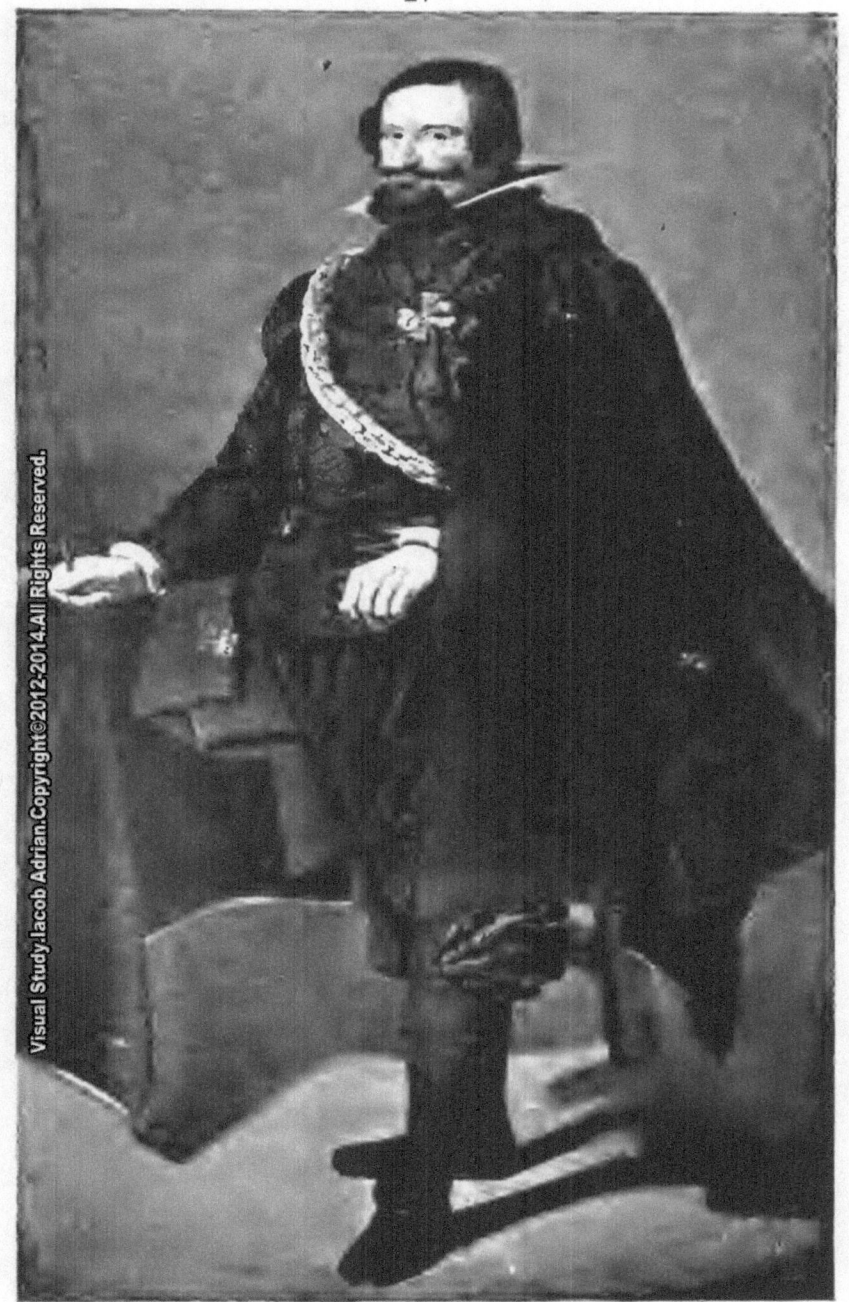

THE DUKE OF OLIVARES
(*Huth Collection*)

LE DUC D'OLIVARÈS
(*Collection Huth*)

DER HERZOG VON OLIVARES
(*Sammlung Huth*)
F. Hanfstaengl, Photo.

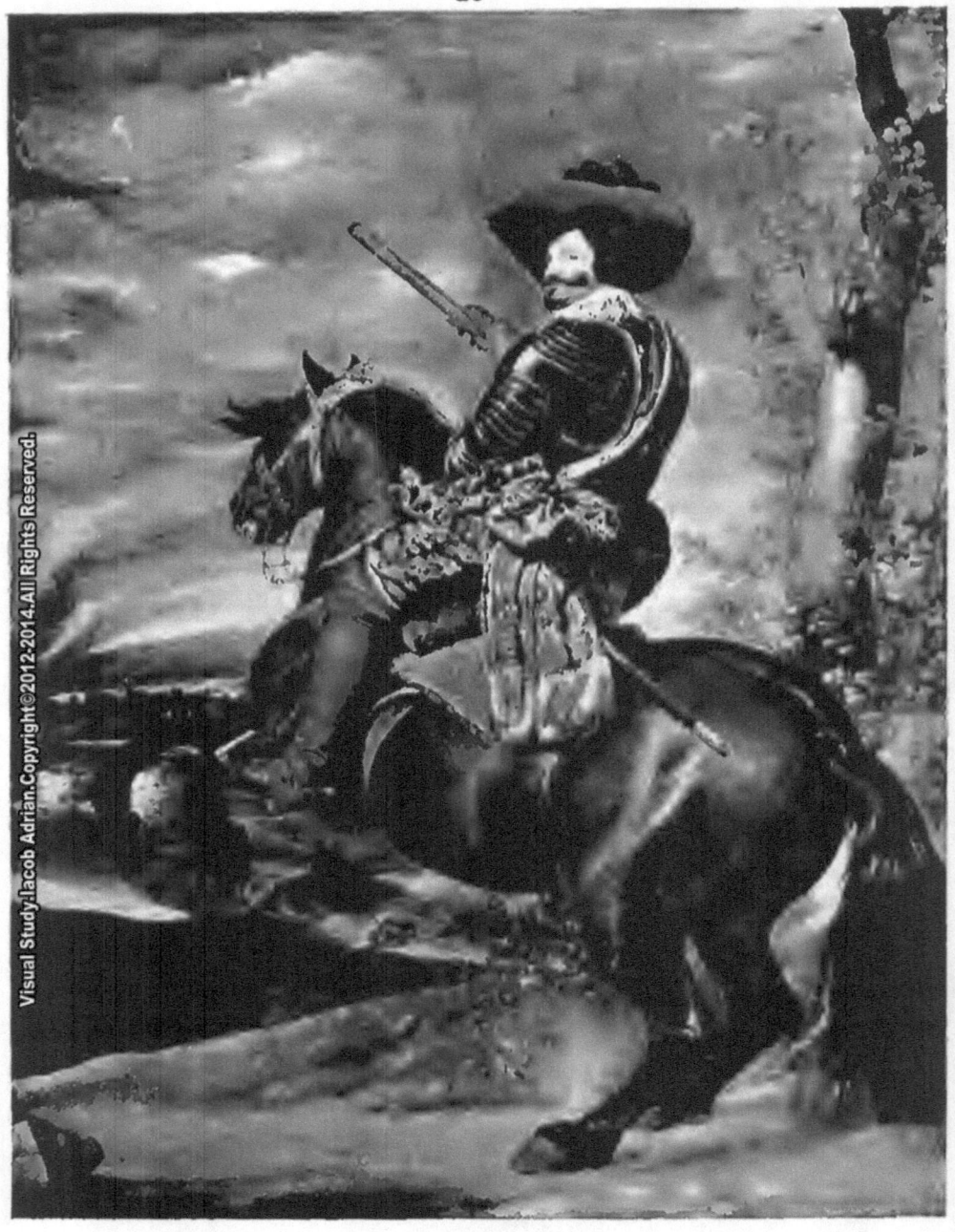

THE DUKE OF OLIVARES   LE DUC D'OLIVARÈS
(*Prado, Madrid*)   (*Prado, Madrid*)
DER HERZOG VON OLIVARES
(*Madrid, Prado*)
D. Anderson, Photo.

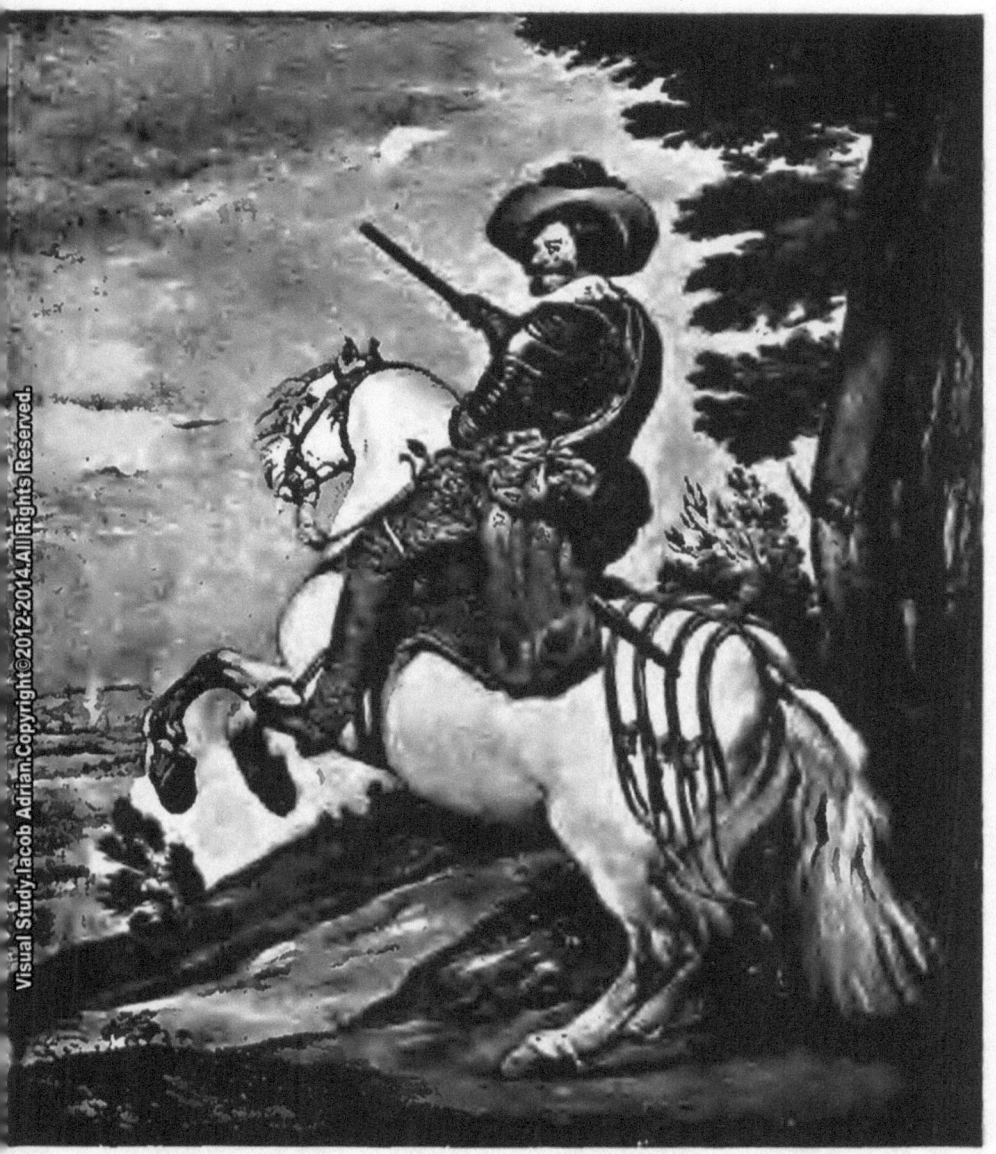

THE DUKE OF OLIVARES   LE DUC D'OLIVARÈS
(*Pinakothek, Munich*)   (*Pinacothèque, Munich*)
DER HERZOG VON OLIVARES
(*München, Pinakothek*)
F. Hanfstaengl, Photo.

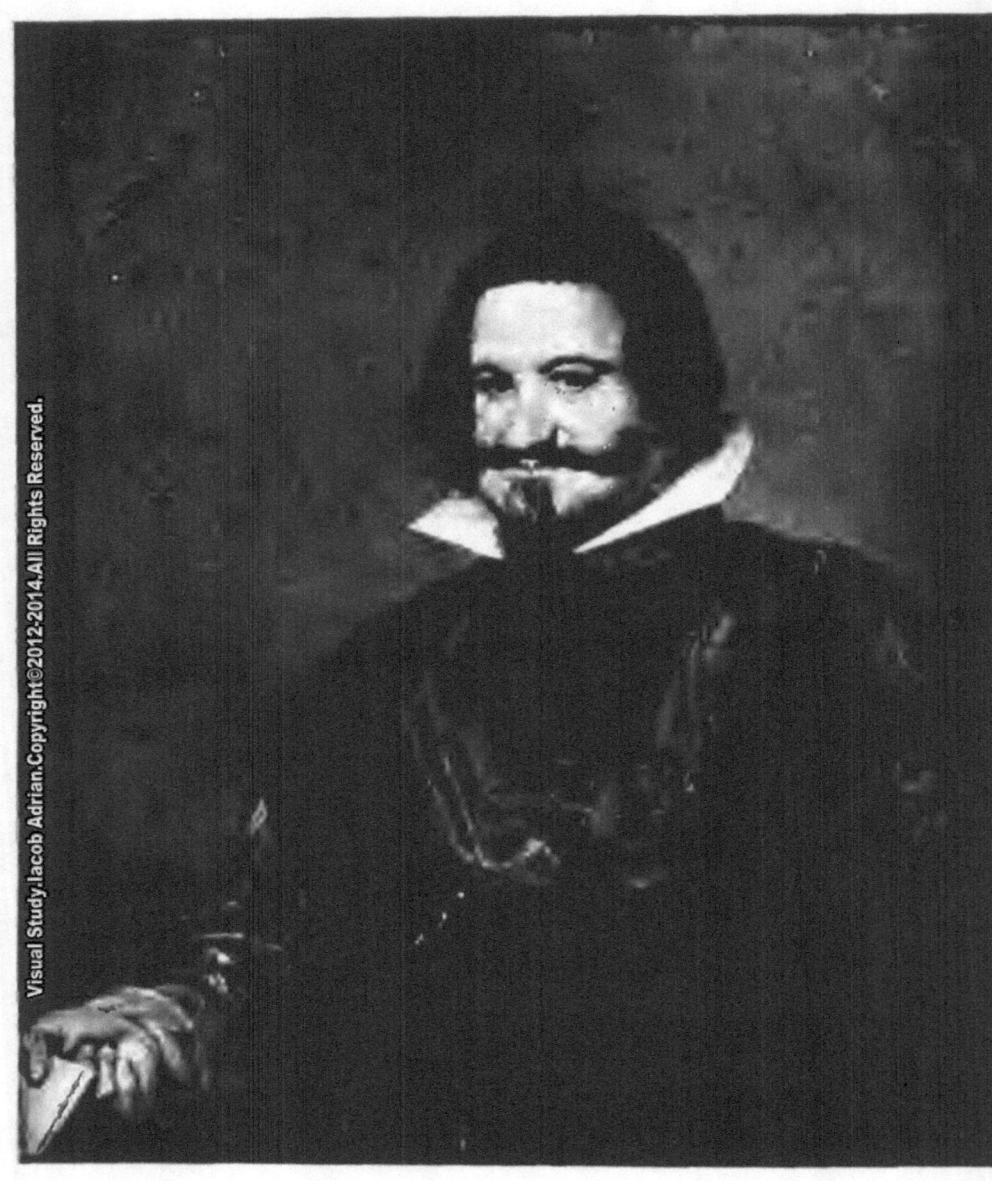

THE DUKE OF OLIVARES   LE DUC D'OLIVARÈS
(Royal Gallery, Dresden)   *(Galerie royale, Dresde)*
DER HERZOG VON OLIVARES
(Dresden, Kgl. Galerie)
F. Hanfstaengl, Photo.

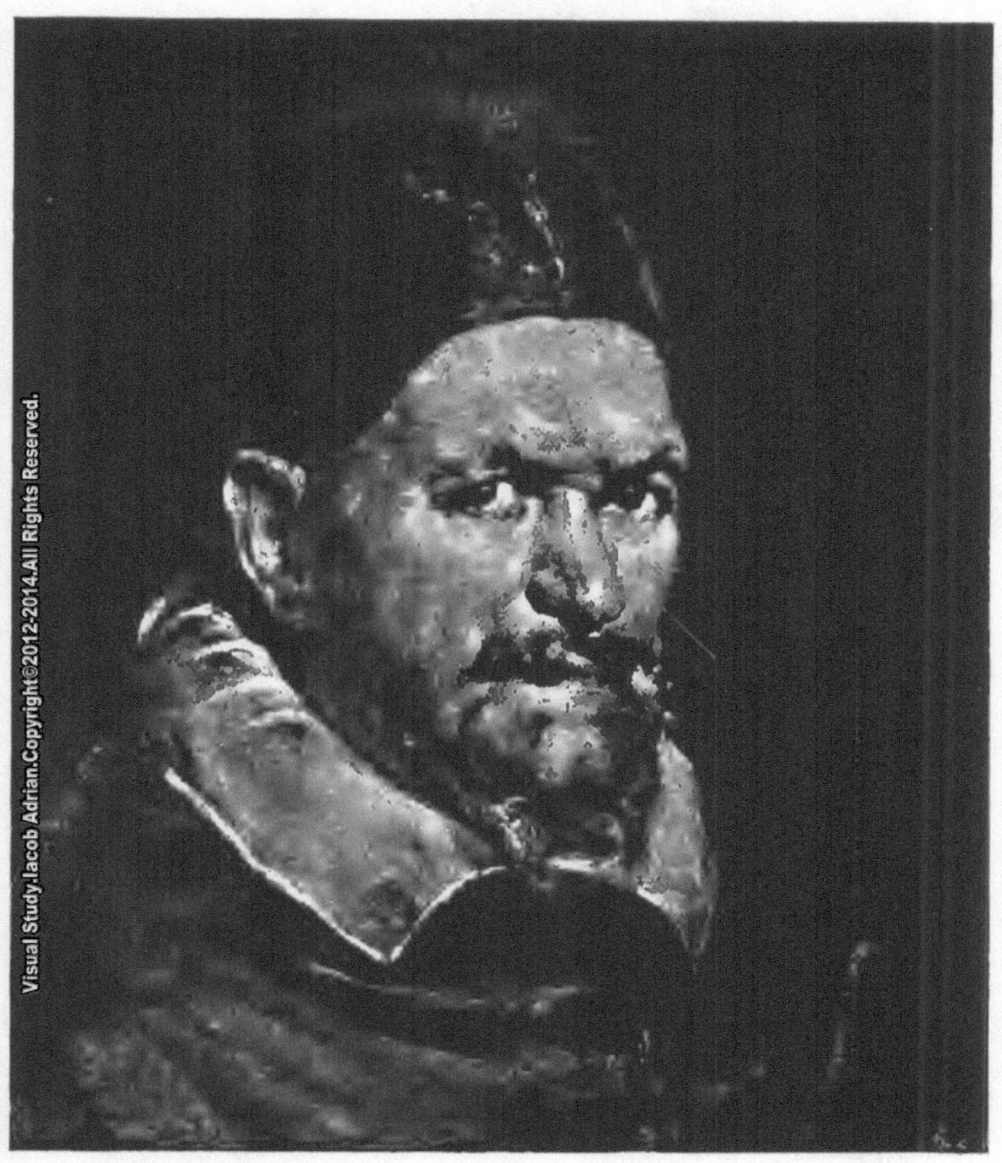

POPE INNOCENT X.   LE PAPE INNOCENT X.

(*The Hermitage, St. Petersburg*) (*L'Ermitage, Saint-Pétersbourg*)

PAPST INNOCENZ X.

(*Petersburg, Eremitage*)

F. Hanfstaengl, Photo.

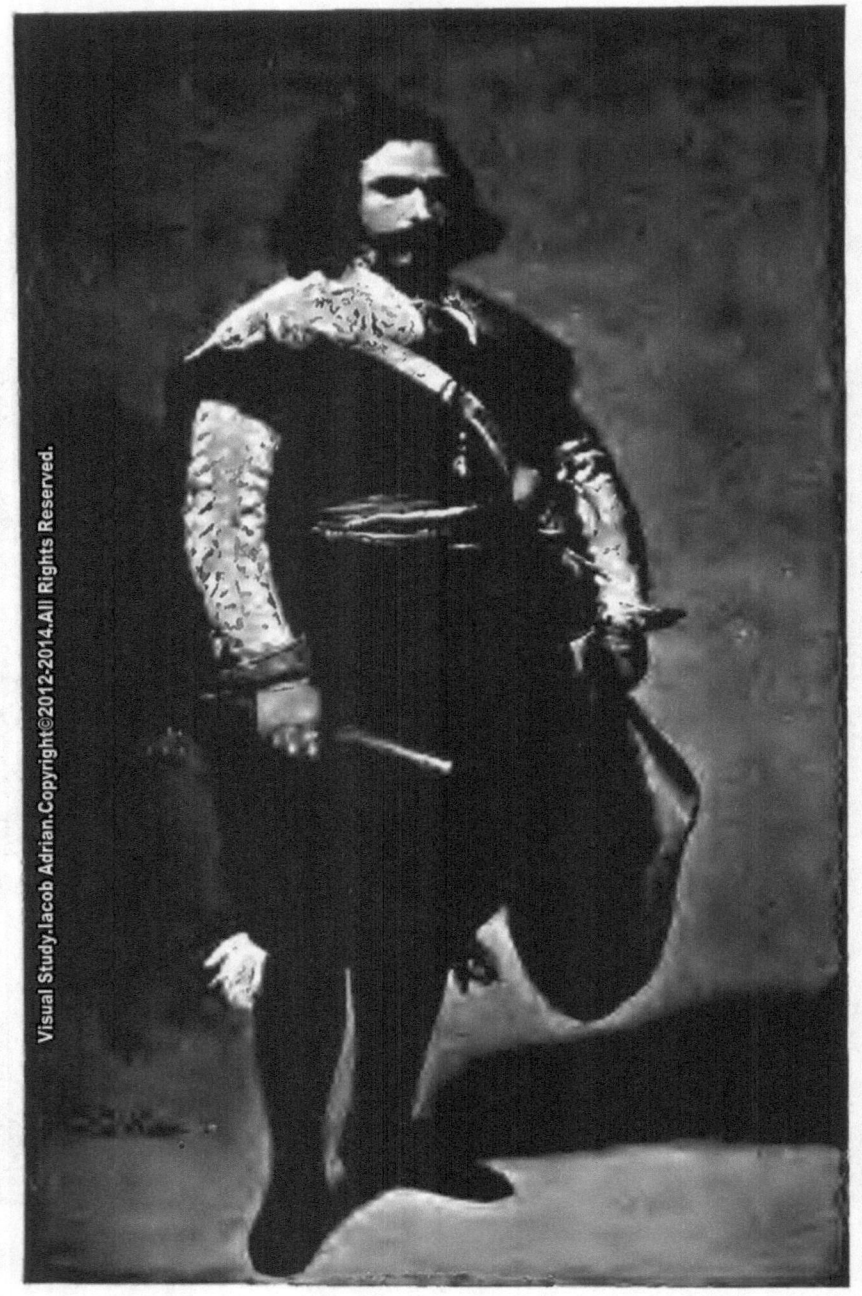

ADMIRAL PULIDO
(*National Gallery, London*)

L'AMIRAL PULIDO
(*Galerie nationale, Londres*)

ADMIRAL PULIDO
(*London, Nationalgalerie*)
· *F. Hanfstaengl, Photo.*

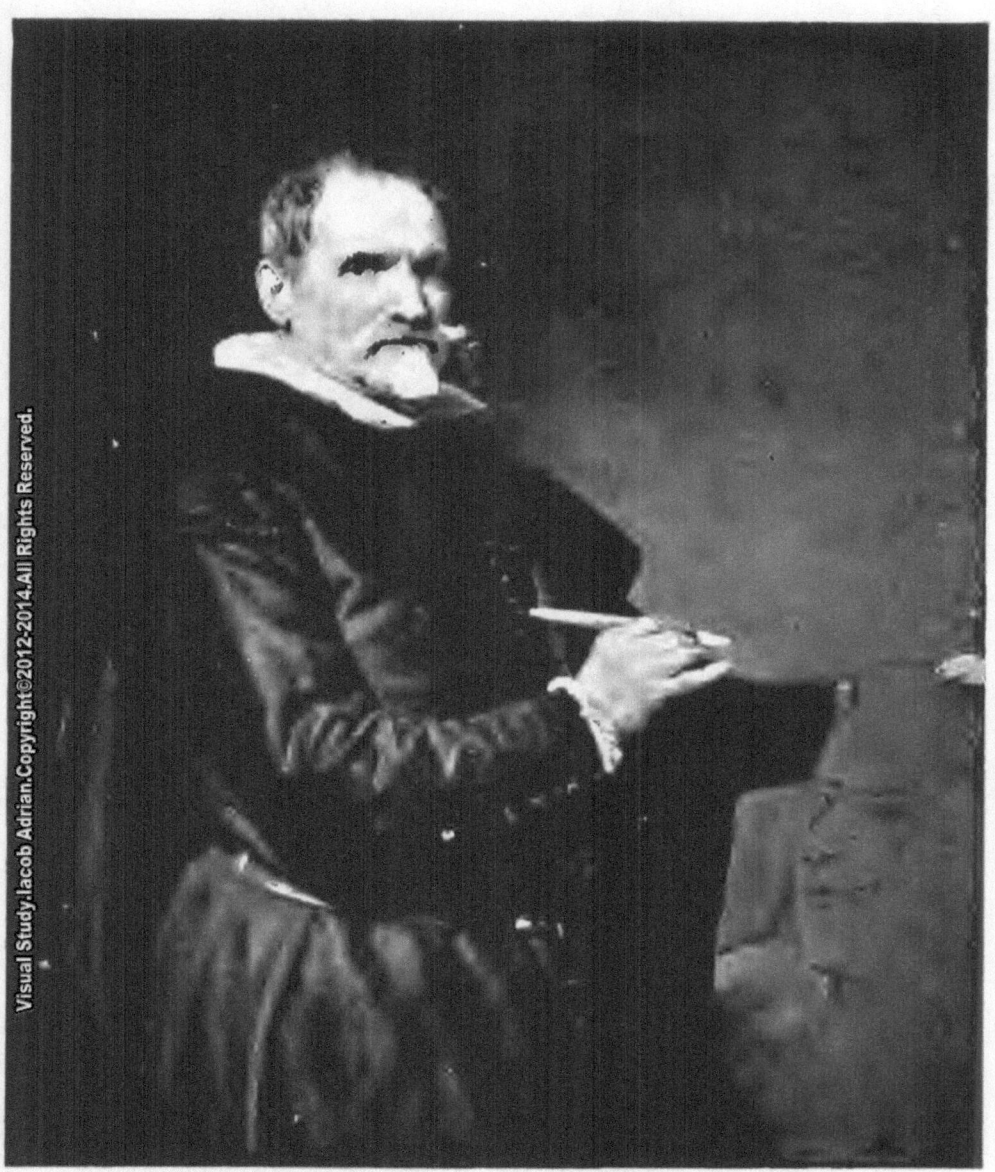

THE SCULPTOR MARTINEZ
MONTAÑES
(*Prado, Madrid*)

LE SCULPTEUR MARTINEZ
MONTAÑES
(*Prado, Madrid*)

DER BILDHAUER MARTINEZ MONTAÑES
(*Madrid, Prado*)
D. Anderson, Photo.

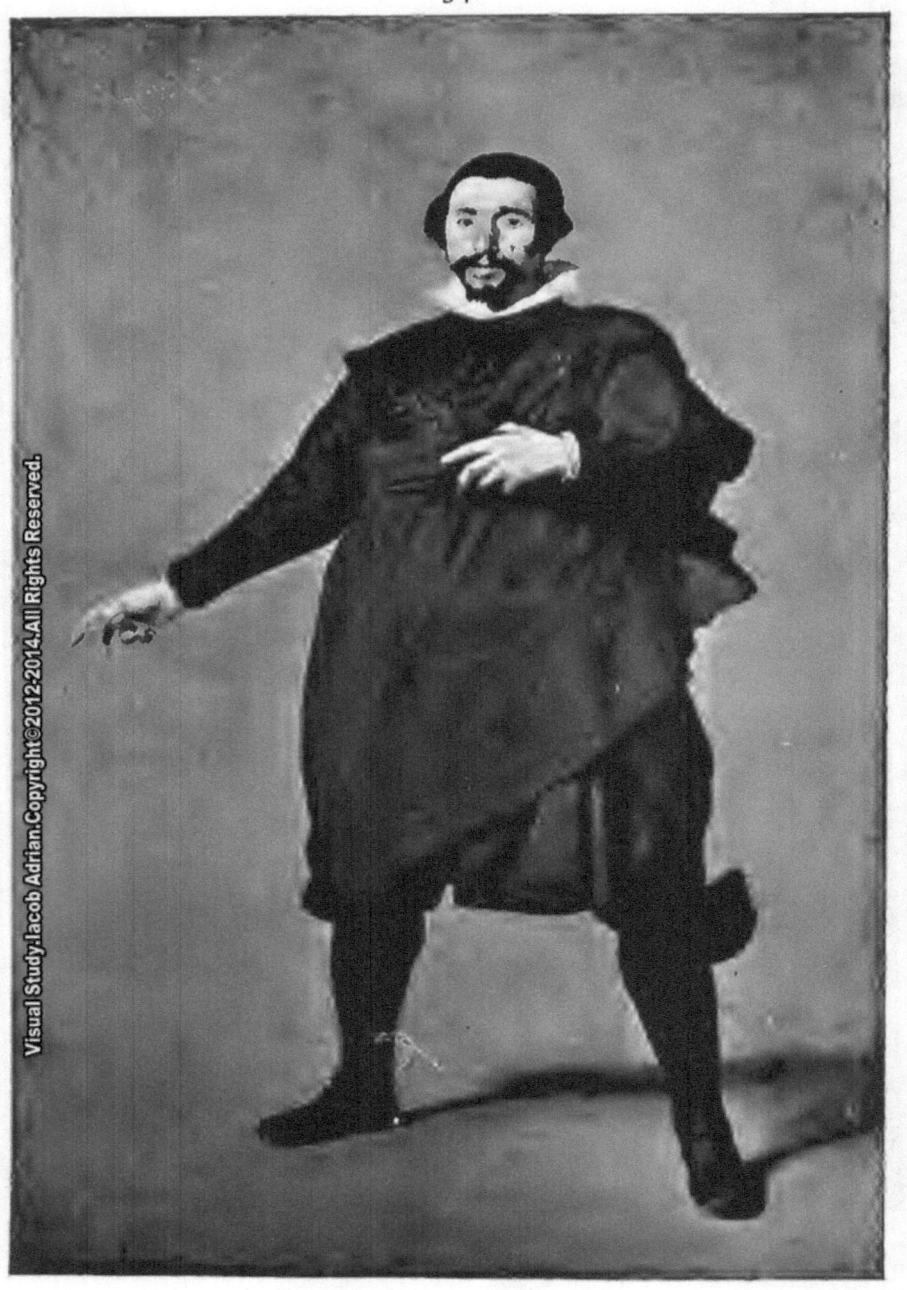

THE BUFFOON,
"PABLILLOS OF VALLADOLID"
(*Prado, Madrid*)

LE BOUFFON,
"PABLILLOS DE VALLADOLID"
(*Prado, Madrid*)

DER HOFNARR "PABLILLOS VON VALLADOLID"
(*Madrid, Prado*)
D. Anderson, Photo.

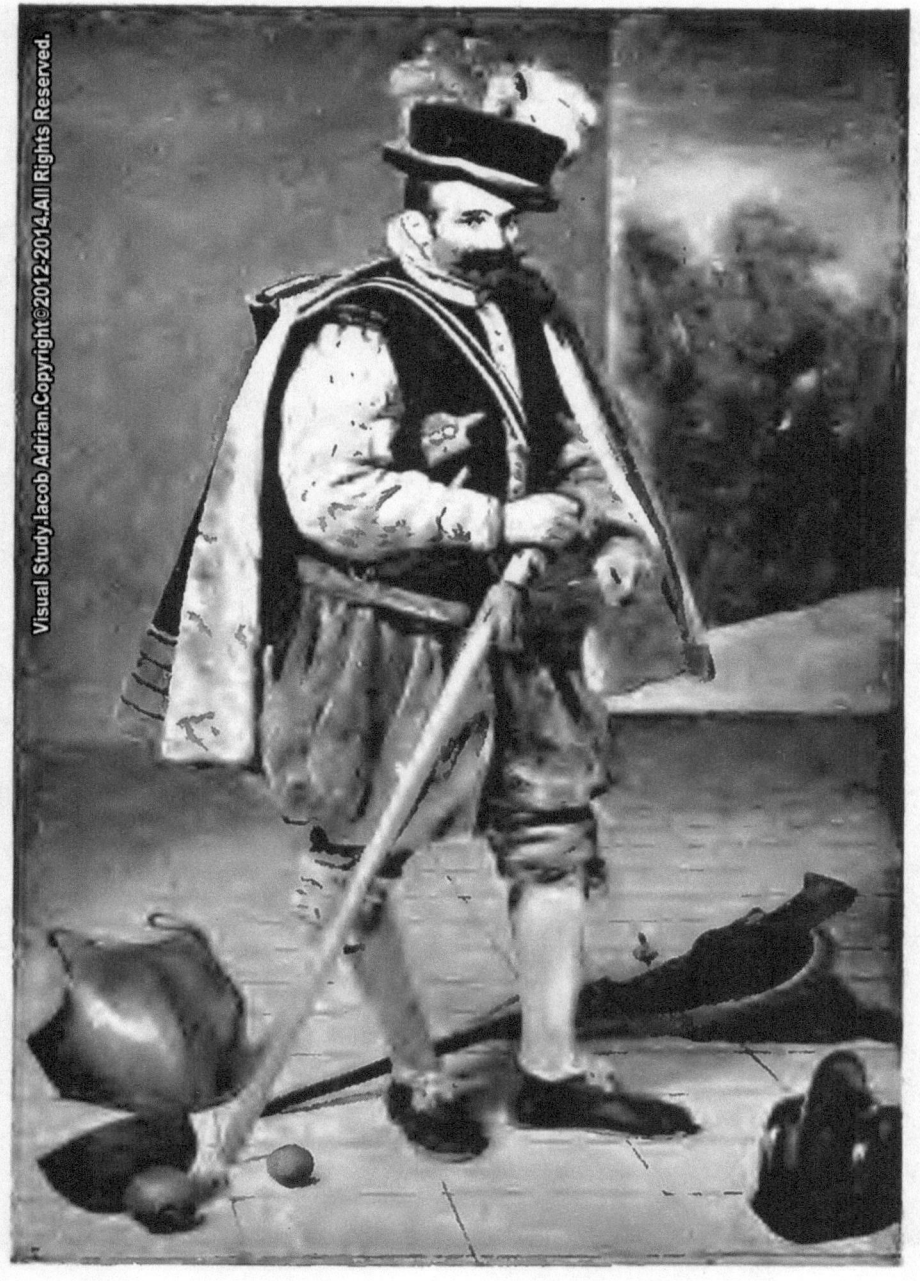

THE BUFFOON,
"DON JOHN OF AUSTRIA"
(*Prado, Madrid*)

LE BOUFFON,
"DON JUAN D'AUTRICHE"
(*Prado, Madrid*)

DER HOFNARR "DON JUAN VON ÖSTERREICH"
(*Madrid, Prado*)
D. Anderson, Photo.

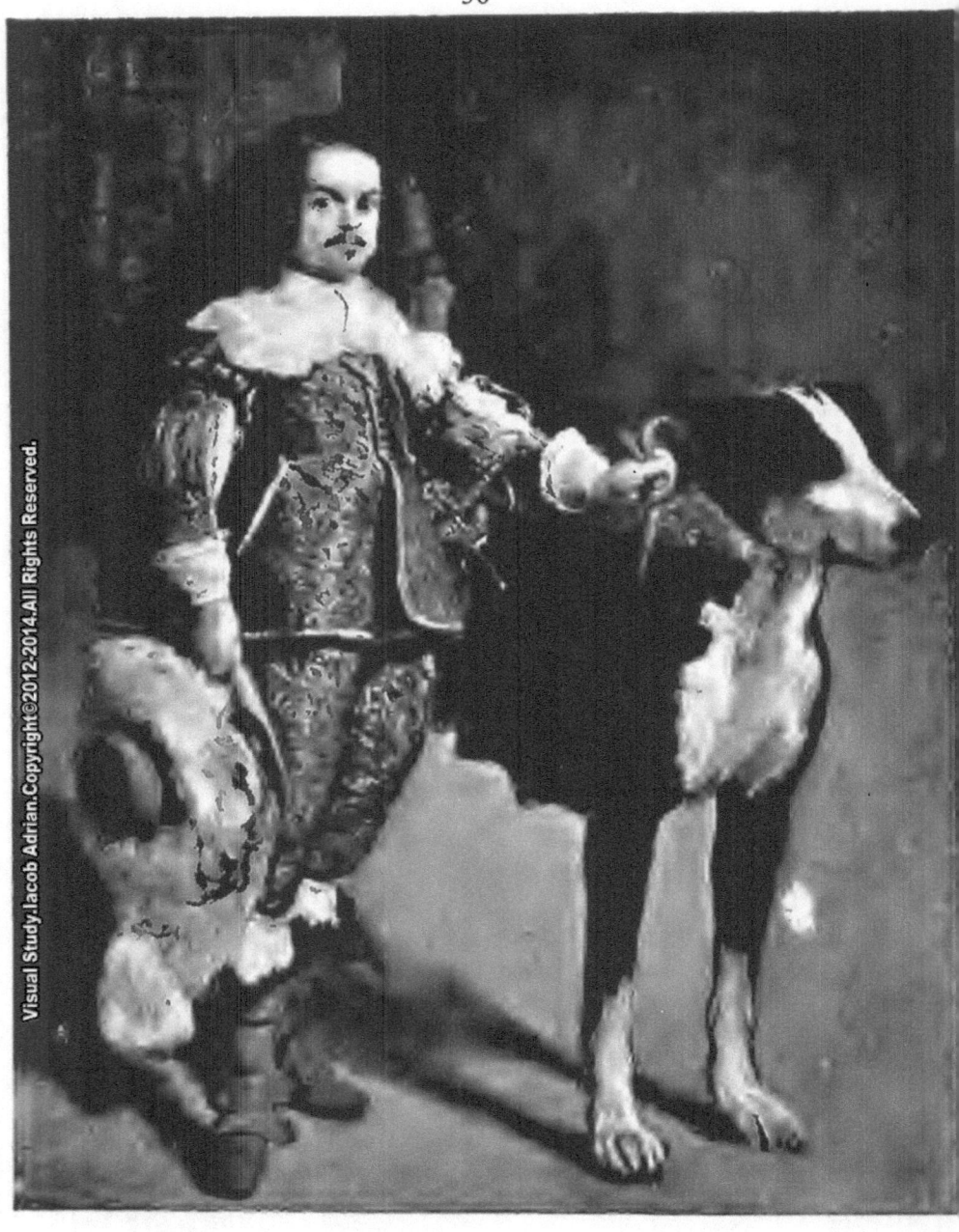

THE DWARF,   LE NAIN,
"DON ANTONIO THE ENGLISHMAN" "DON ANTONIO L'ANGLAIS"
(*Prado, Madrid*)   (*Prado, Madrid*)
DER HOFZWERG "DON ANTONIO DER ENGLÄNDER"
(*Madrid, Prado*)
D. Anderson, Photo.

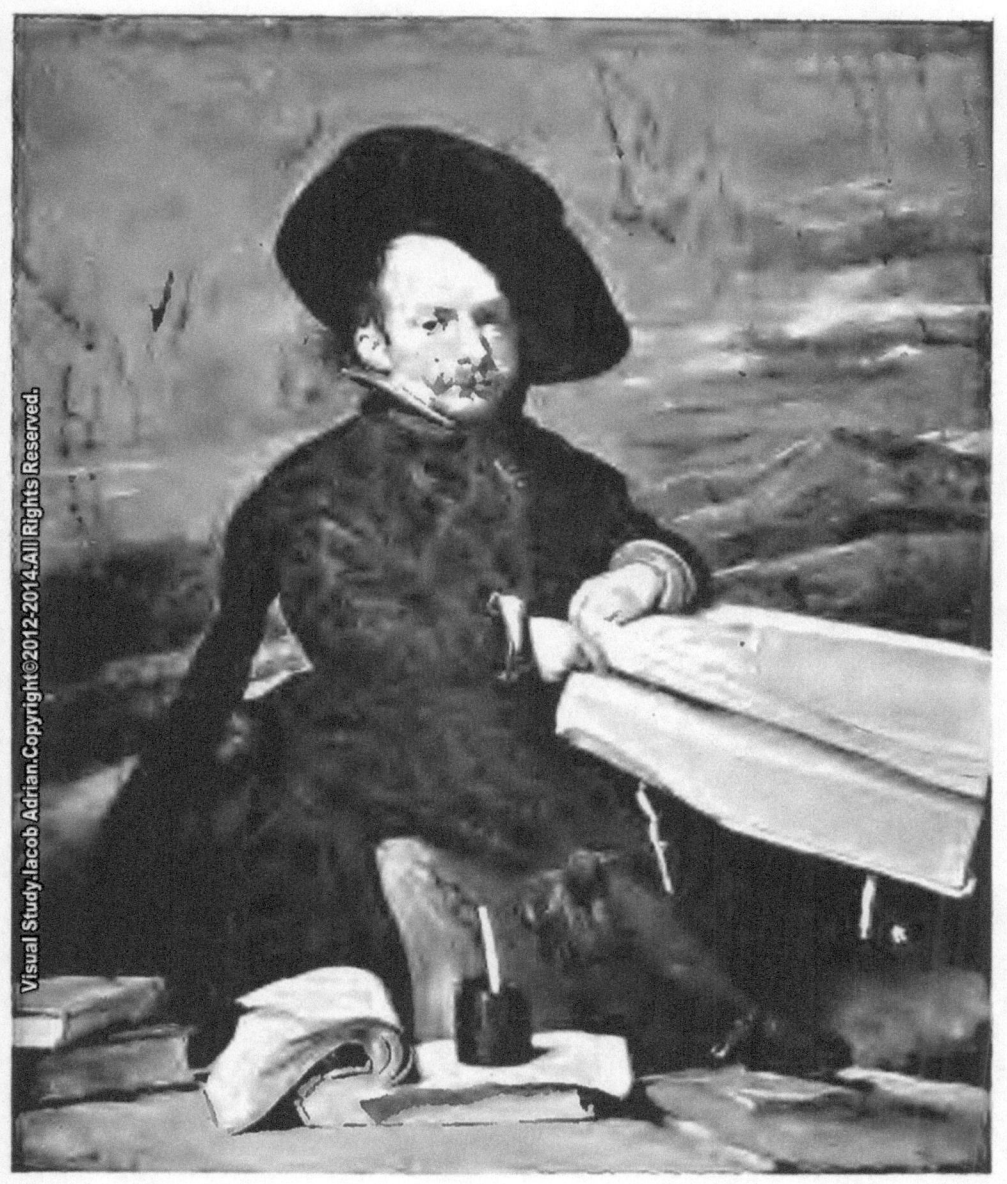

THE DWARF, "EL PRIMO"   LE NAIN, "EL PRIMO"
(*Prado, Madrid*)   (*Prado, Madrid*)
DER HOFZWERG "EL PRIMO"
(*Madrid, Prado*)
D. Anderson, Photo.

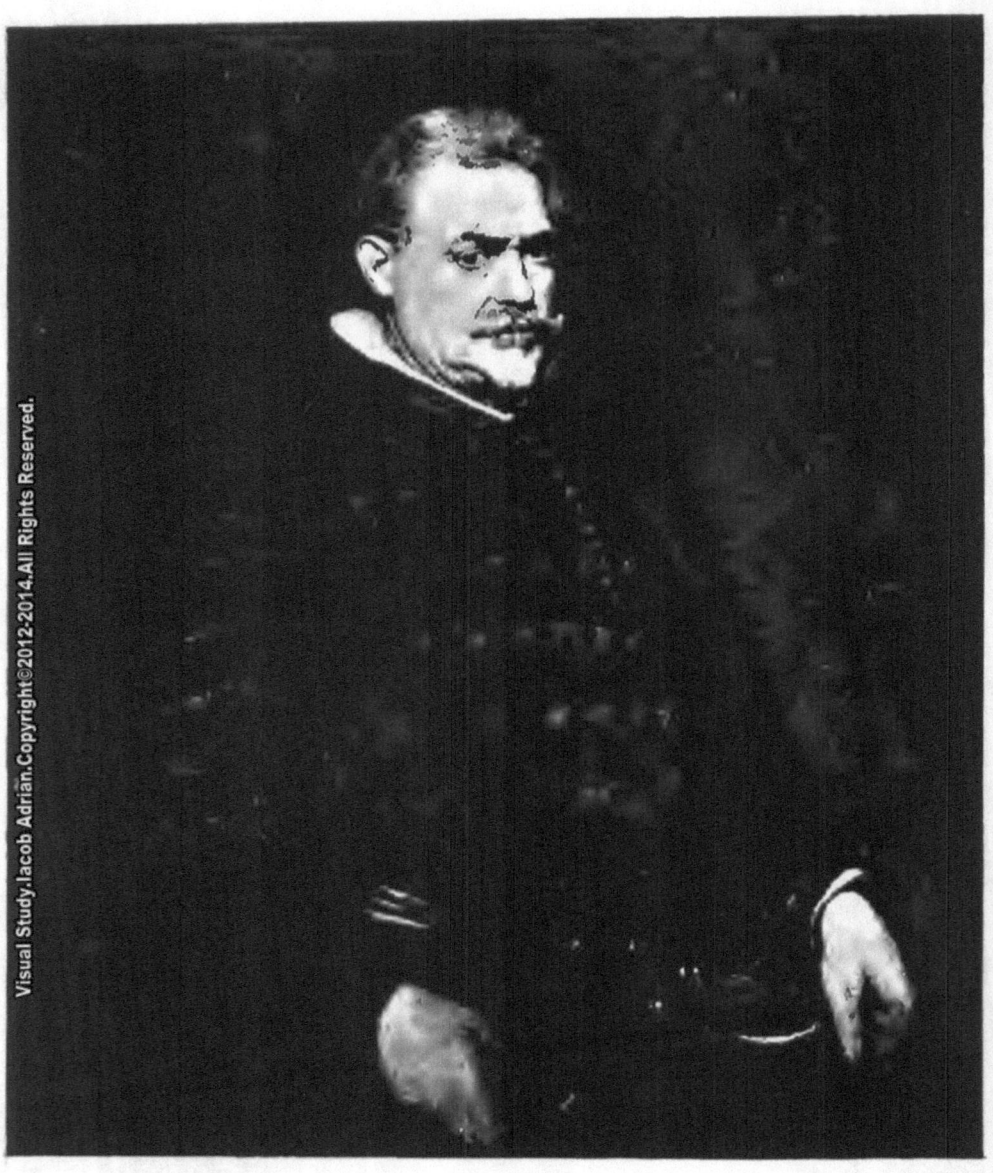

PORTRAIT OF A MAN   PORTRAIT D'HOMME
(*Royal Gallery, Dresden*)   (*Galerie royale, Dresde*)

BILDNIS EINES MANNES
(*Dresden, Kgl. Galerie*)
F. Hanfstaengl, Photo.

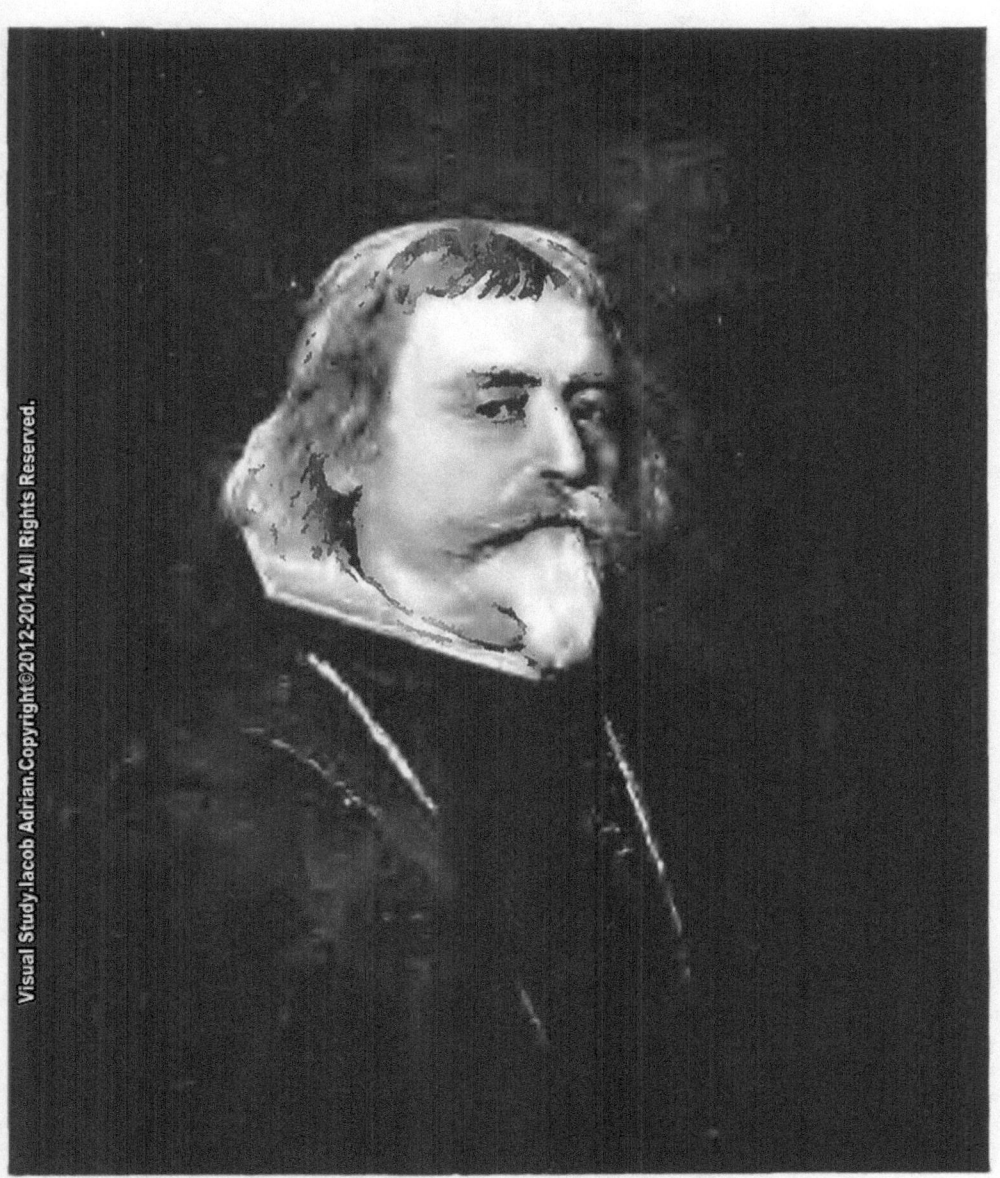

PORTRAIT OF AN OLD MAN   PORTRAIT D'UN HOMME AGÉ
(Royal Gallery, Dresden)   (Galerie royale, Dresde)
BILDNIS EINES ALTEN MANNES
(Dresden, Kgl. Galerie)
F. Hanfstaengl, Photo.

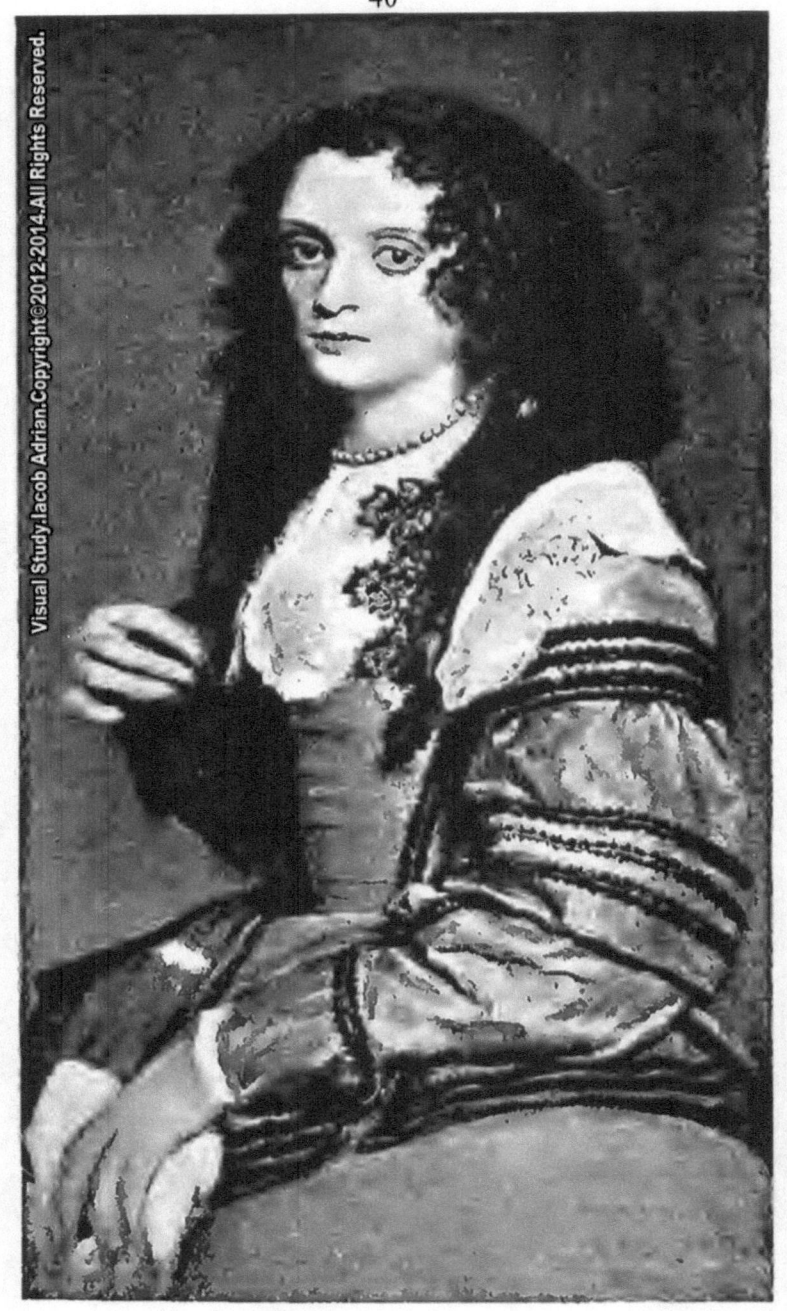

PORTRAIT OF A LADY   PORTRAIT DE DAME
(*Duke of Devonshire, London*)   (*Duc de Devonshire, Londres*)
BILDNIS EINER DAME
(*London, Herzog von Devonshire*)
F. Hanfstaengl, Photo.

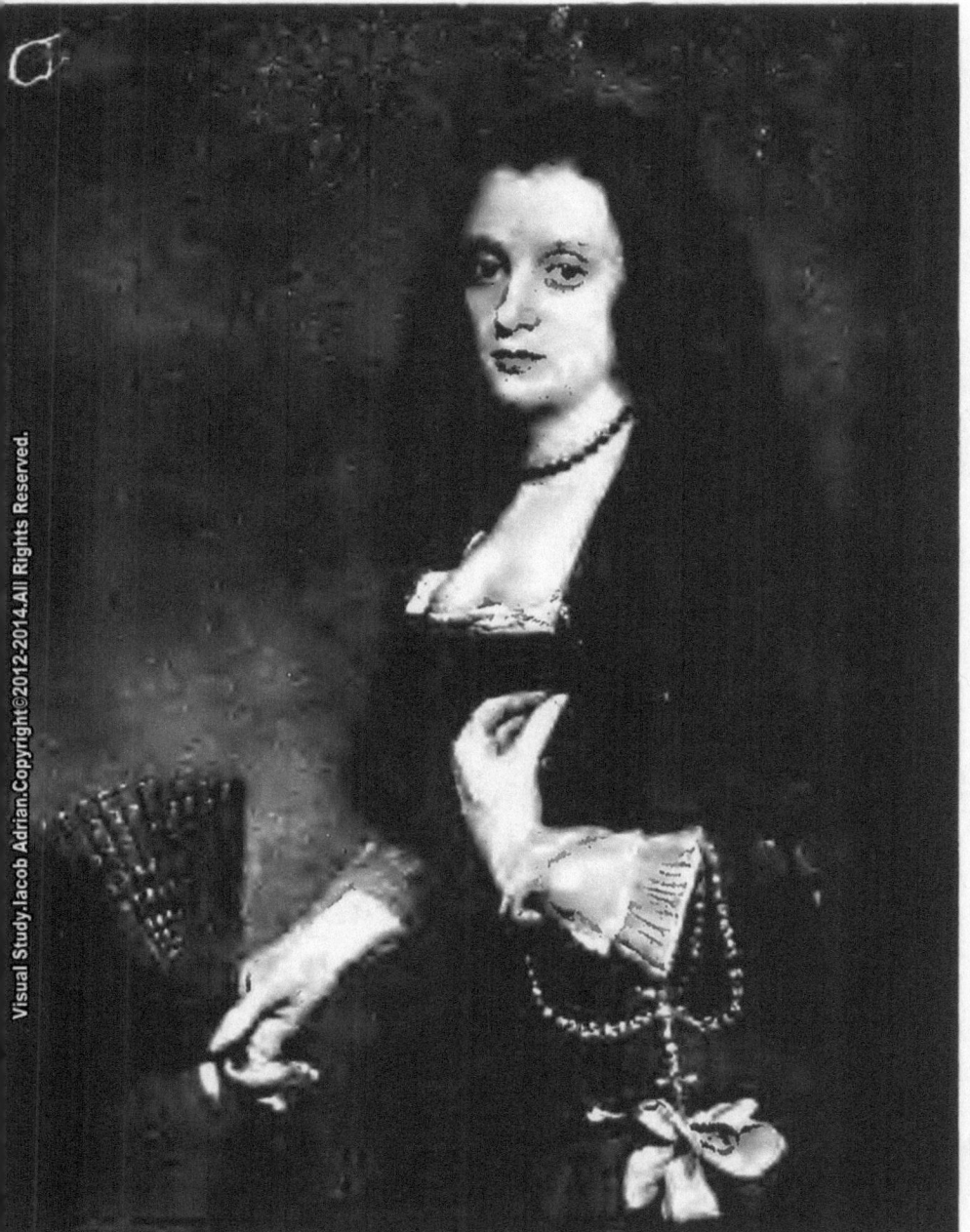

PORTRAIT OF A LADY   PORTRAIT DE DAME
(*Wallace Collection, London*)   (*Collection Wallace, Londres*)
BILDNIS EINER DAME
(*London, Sammlung Wallace*)
F. Hanfstaengl, Photo.

42

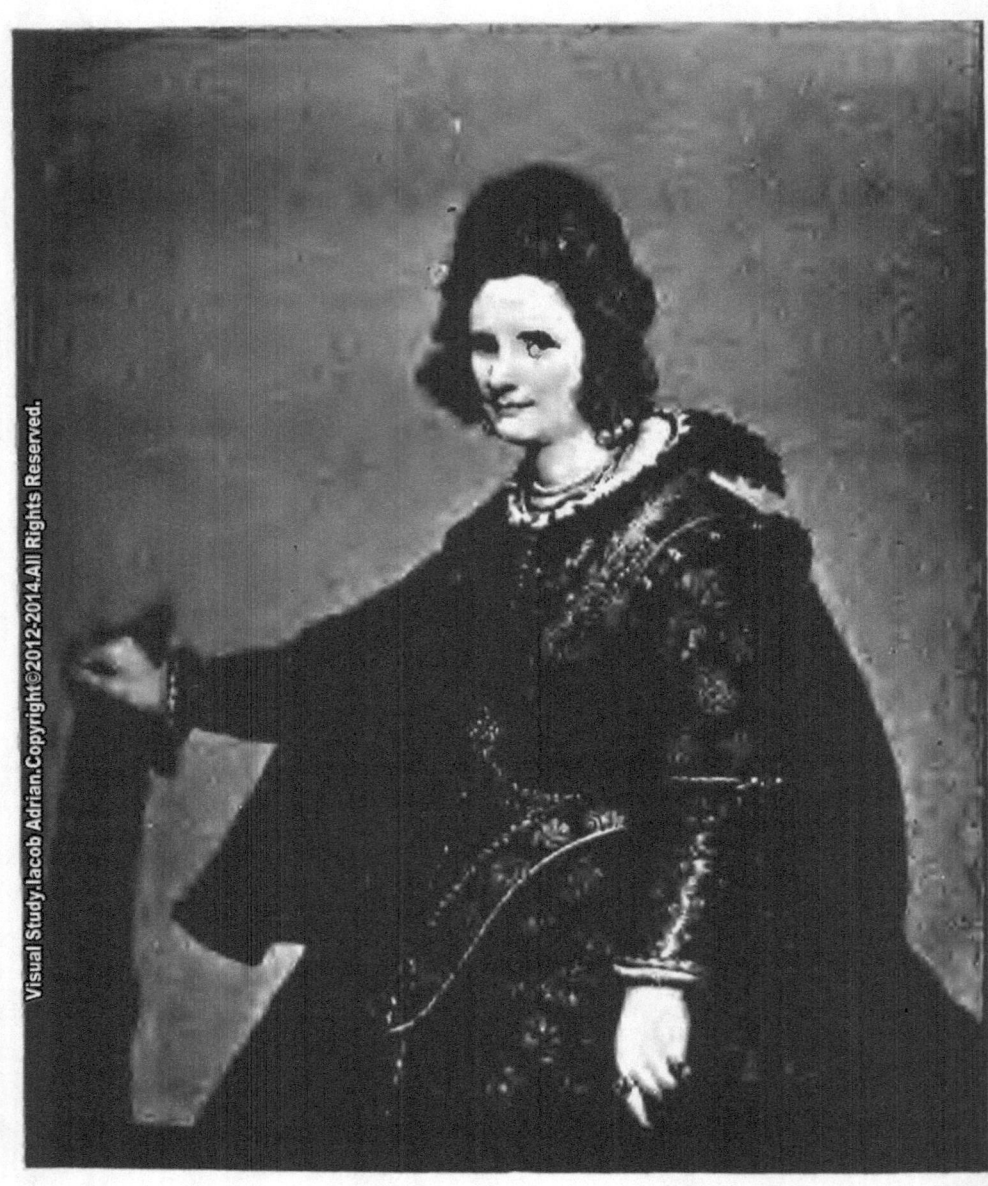

PORTRAIT OF A LADY   PORTRAIT DE DAME
(Royal Gallery, Berlin)   *(Musée royal, Berlin)*
BILDNIS EINER DAME
(Berlin, Kgl. Galerie)
F. Hanfstaengl, Photo.

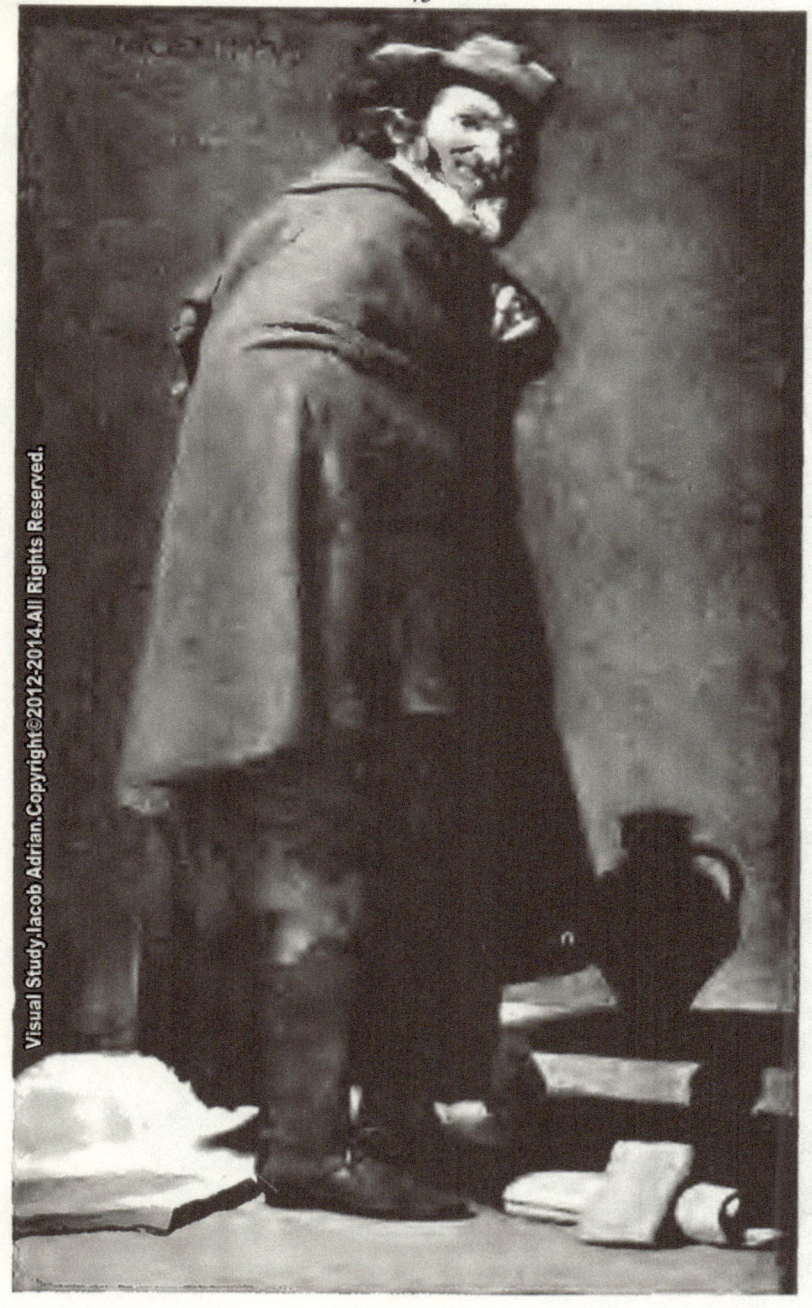

MENIPPUS
(*Prado, Madrid*)

MÉNIPPE
(*Prado, Madrid*)

MENIPPUS
(*Madrid, Prado*)
D. Anderson, Photo.

44

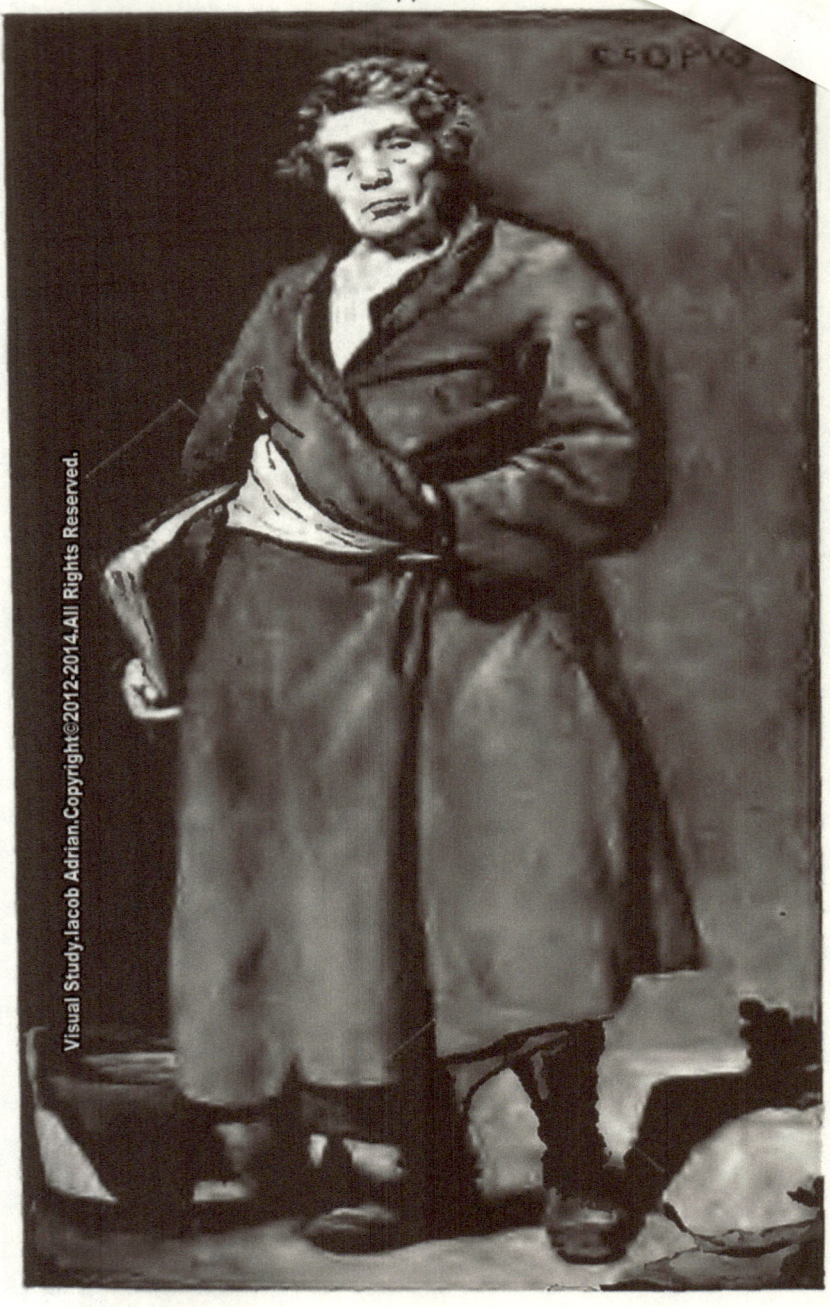

ÆSOP
(*Prado, Madrid*)

ÉSOPE
(*Prado, Madrid*)

ÄSOP
(*Madrid, Prado*)
D. Anderson, Photo.

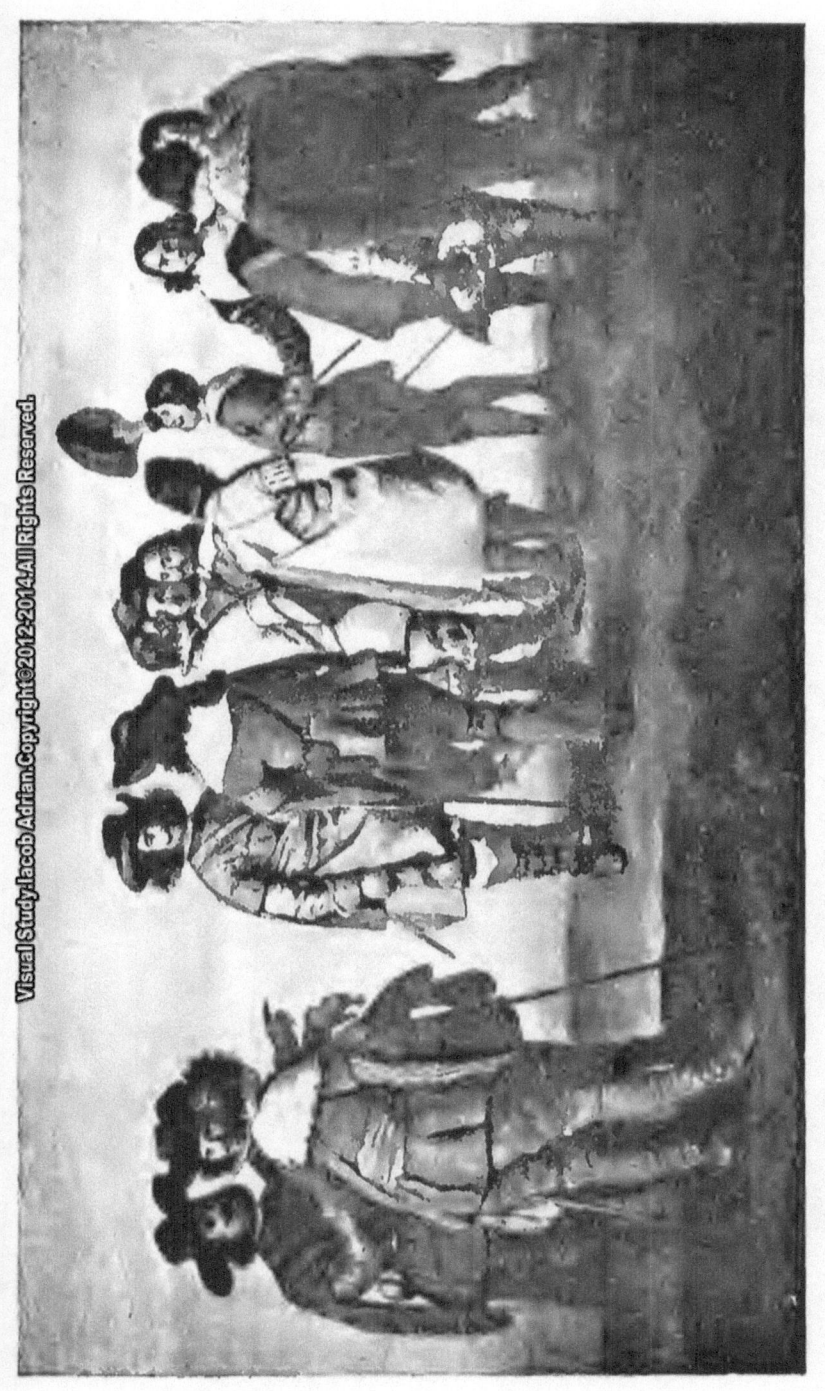

A GROUP OF THIRTEEN GENTLEMEN
(*Louvre, Paris*)

GROUPE DE TREIZE GENTILSHOMMES
(*Louvre, Paris*)

EINE GRUPPE VON DREIZEHN HERREN
(*Paris, Louvre*)
F. Hanfstaengl, Photo.

46

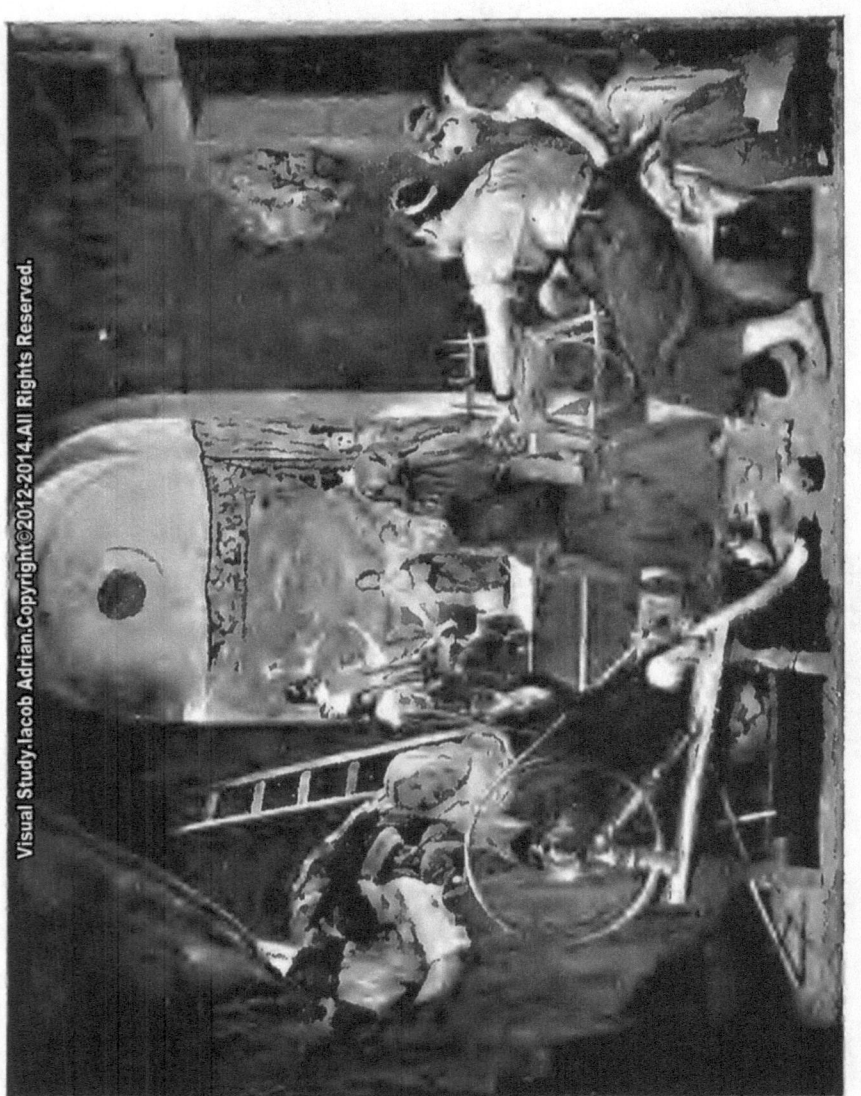

THE SPINNERS
(*Prado, Madrid*)

DIE SPINNERINNEN
(*Madrid, Prado*)
D. Anderson, Photo.

LES FILEUSES
(*Prado, Madrid*)

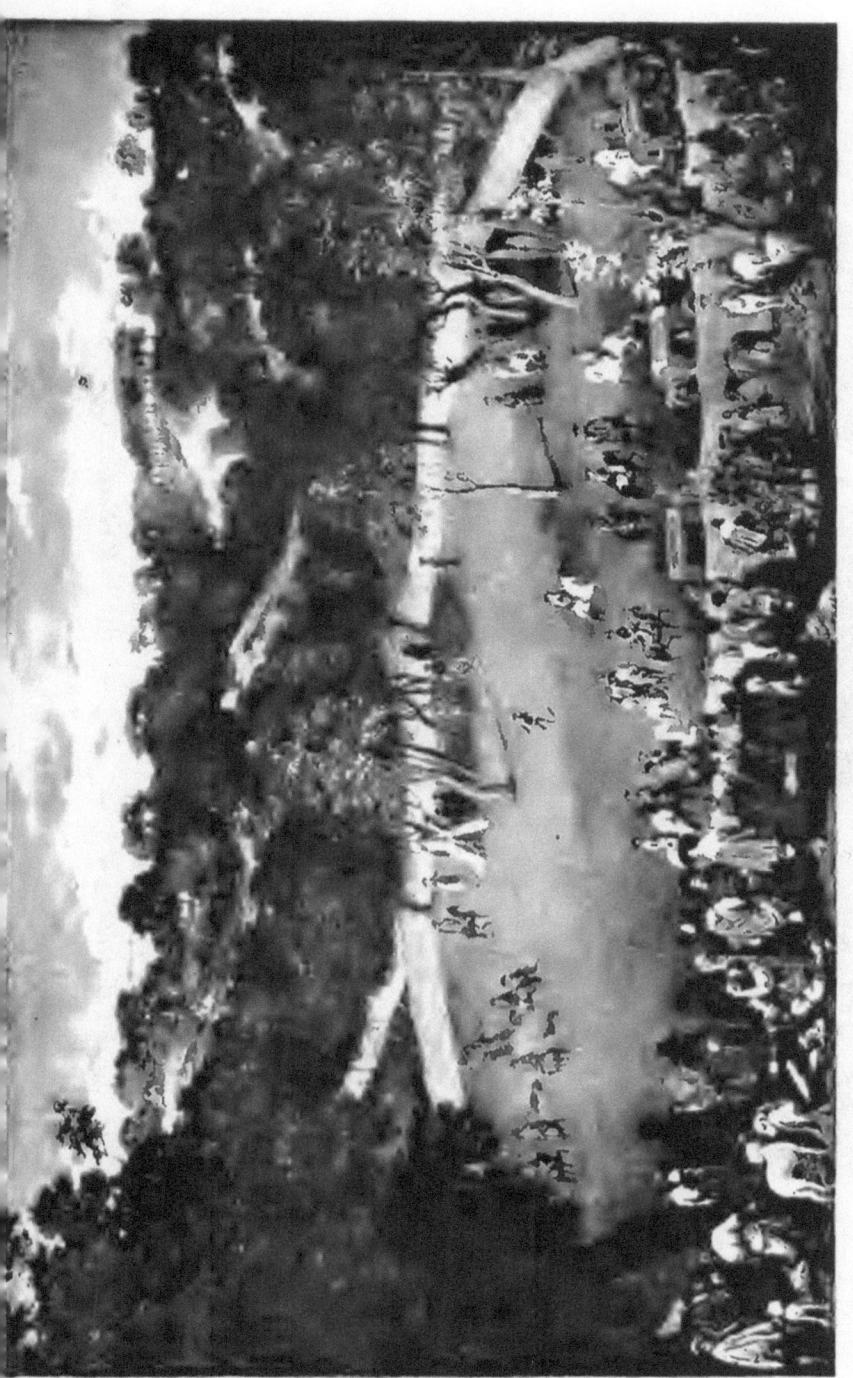

THE BOAR HUNT
(National Gallery, London)

DIE EBERJAGD
(London, Nationalgalerie)
F. Hanfstaengl, Photo.

LA CHASSE AU SANGLIER
(Galerie nationale, Londres)

48

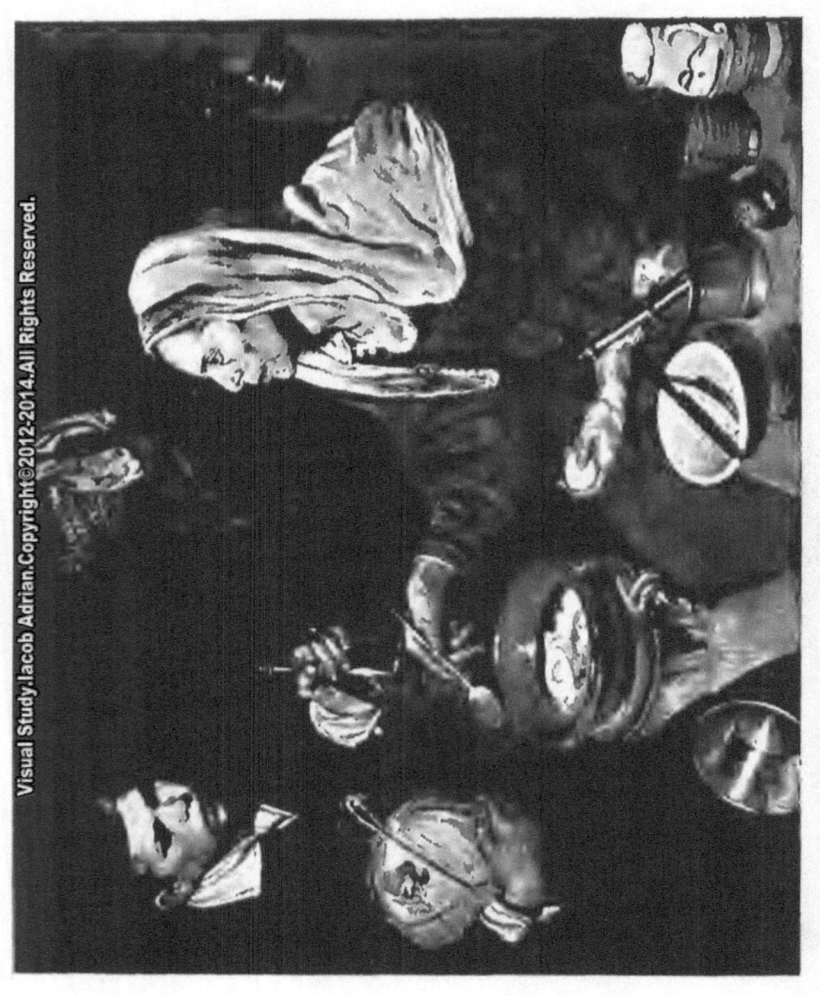

PREPARING AN OMELET
(Cook Collection)

PRÉPARATION D'UNE OMELETTE
(Collection Cook)

ZUBEREITUNG EINES OMELETTS
(Sammlung Cook)

F. Hanfstaengl, Photo.

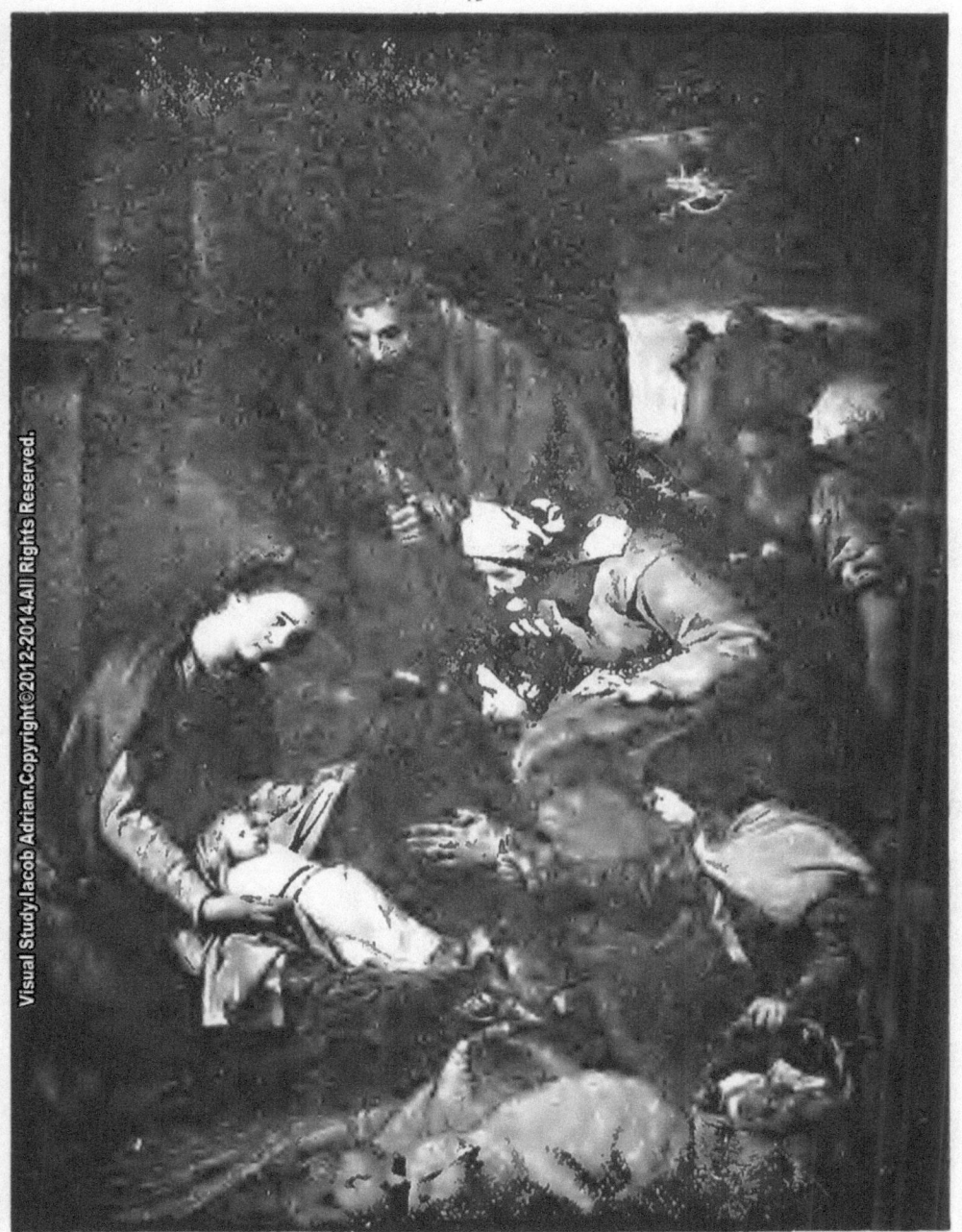

THE ADORATION OF THE SHEPHERDS   L'ADORATION DES BERGERS
(*National Gallery, London*)   (*Galerie nationale, Londres*)
DIE ANBETUNG DER HIRTEN
(*London, Nationalgalerie*)
F. Hanfstaengl, Photo.

50

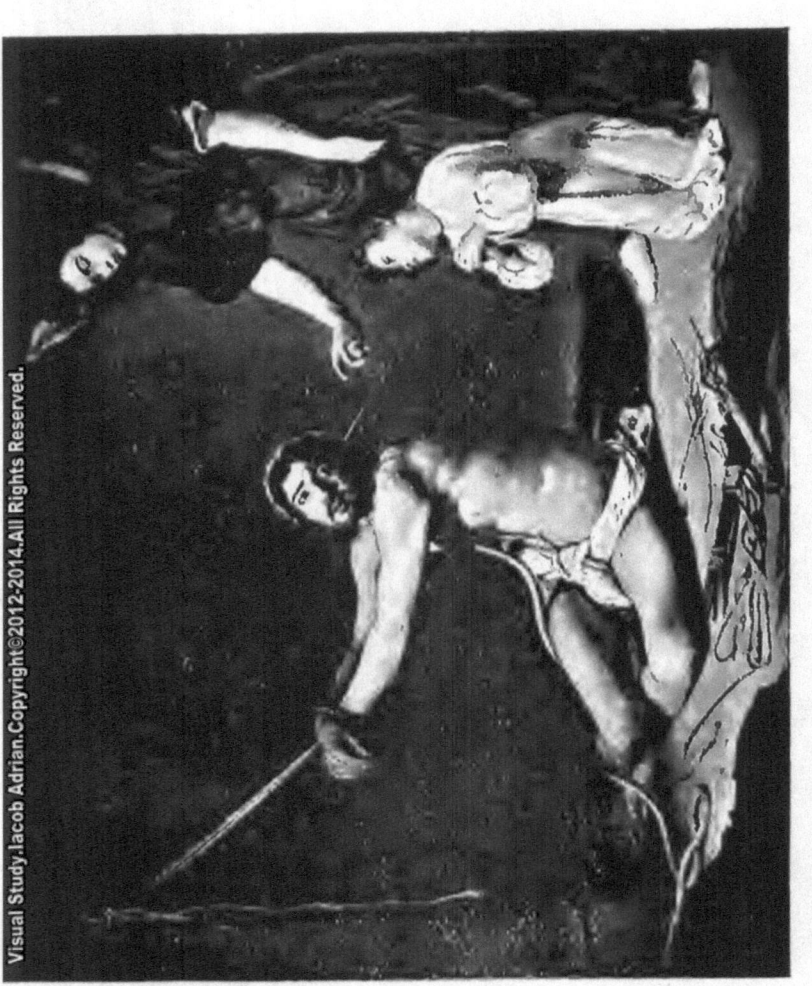

CHRIST AT THE PILLAR
(*National Gallery, London*)

LE CHRIST A LA COLONNE
(*Galerie nationale, Londres*)

CHRISTUS AN DER GEISSEL
(*London, Nationalgalerie*)
F. Hanfstaengl, Photo.

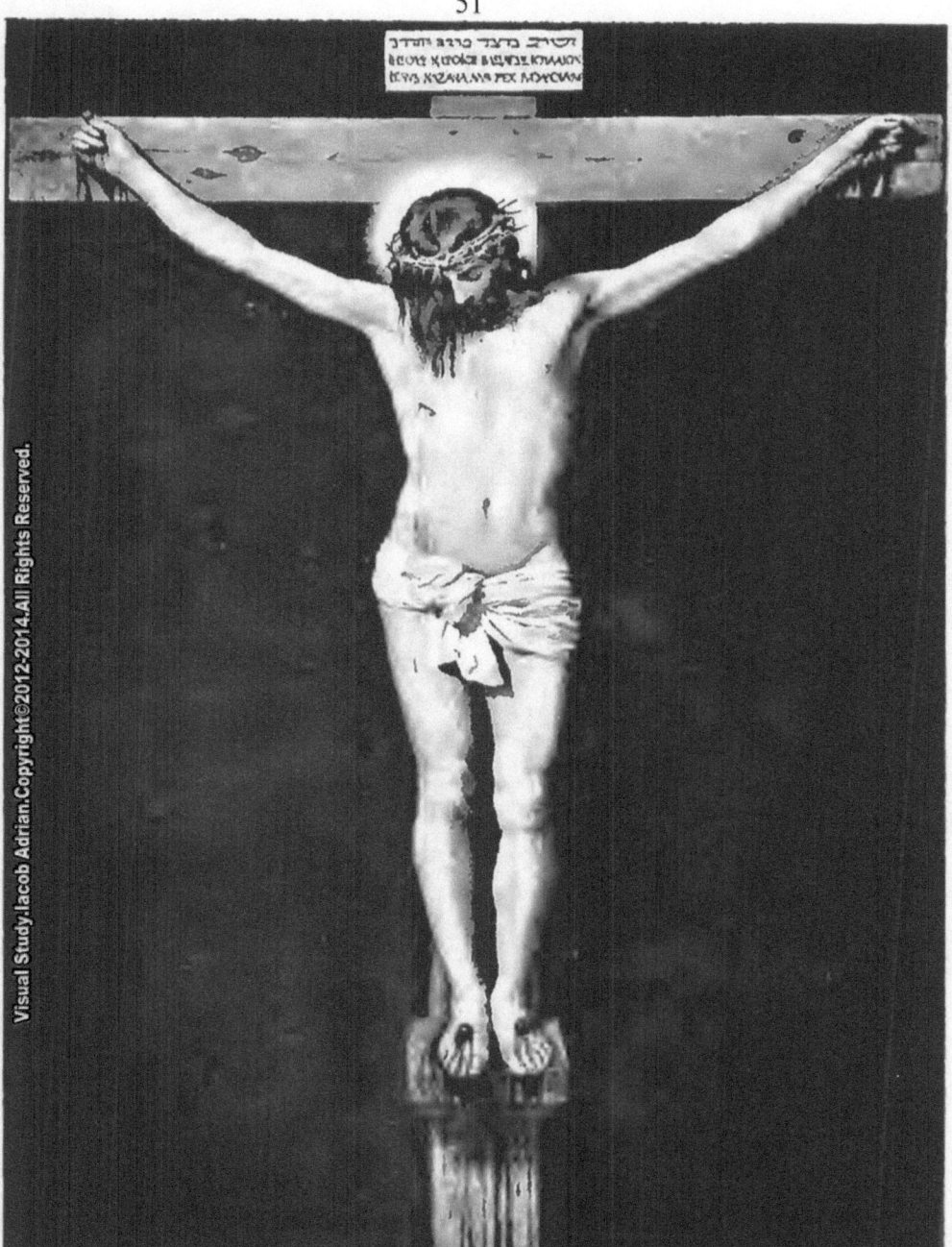

THE CRUCIFIXION
(*Prado, Madrid*)

LE CHRIST SUR LA CROIX
(*Prado, Madrid*)

CHRISTUS AM KREUZ
(*Madrid, Prado*)
D. Anderson, Photo.

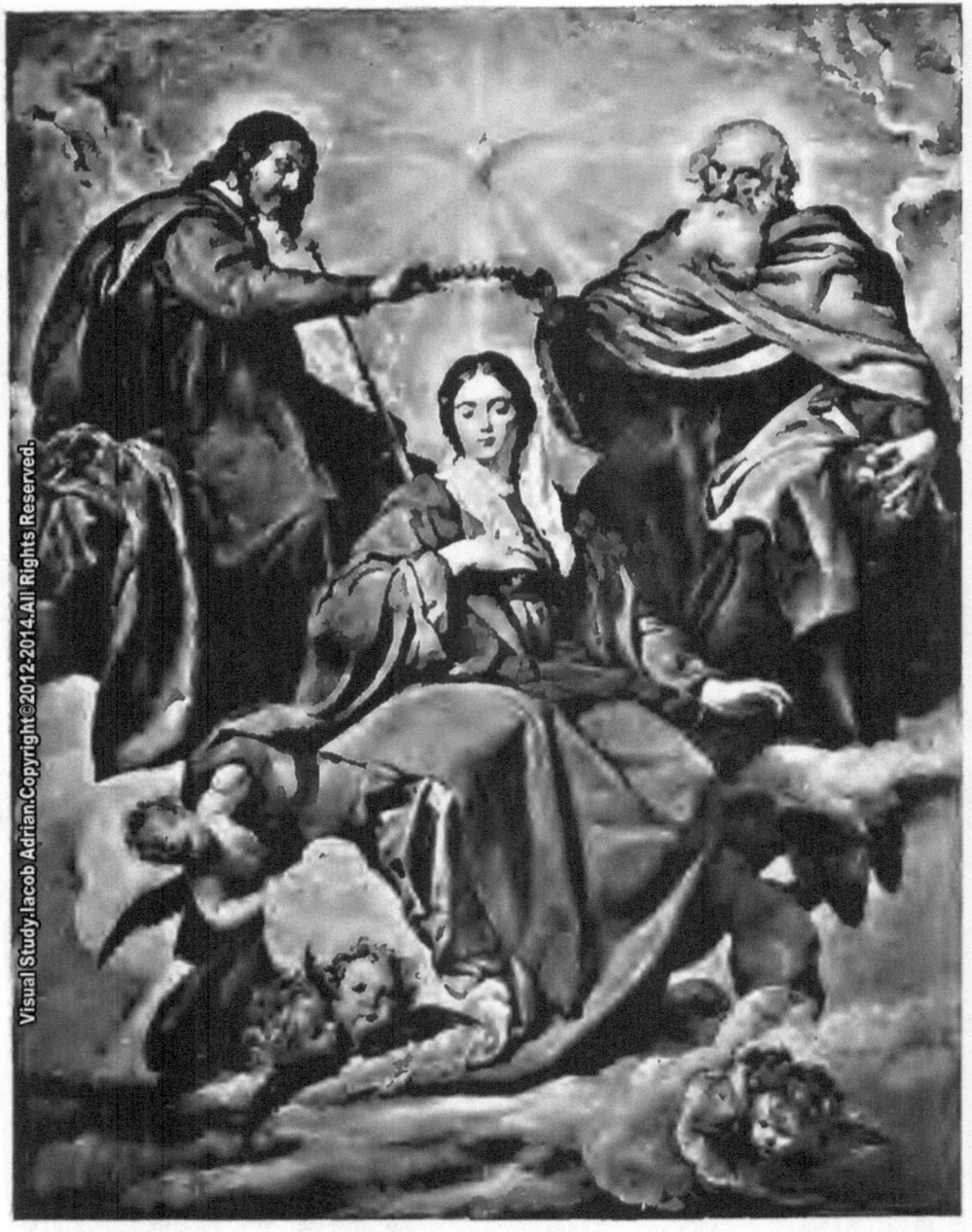

THE CORONATION OF THE   LE COURONNEMENT DE LA
VIRGIN   VIERGE
(*Prado, Madrid*)   (*Prado, Madrid*)

DIE KRÖNUNG MARIÄ
(*Madrid, Prado*)
D. Anderson, Photo.

53

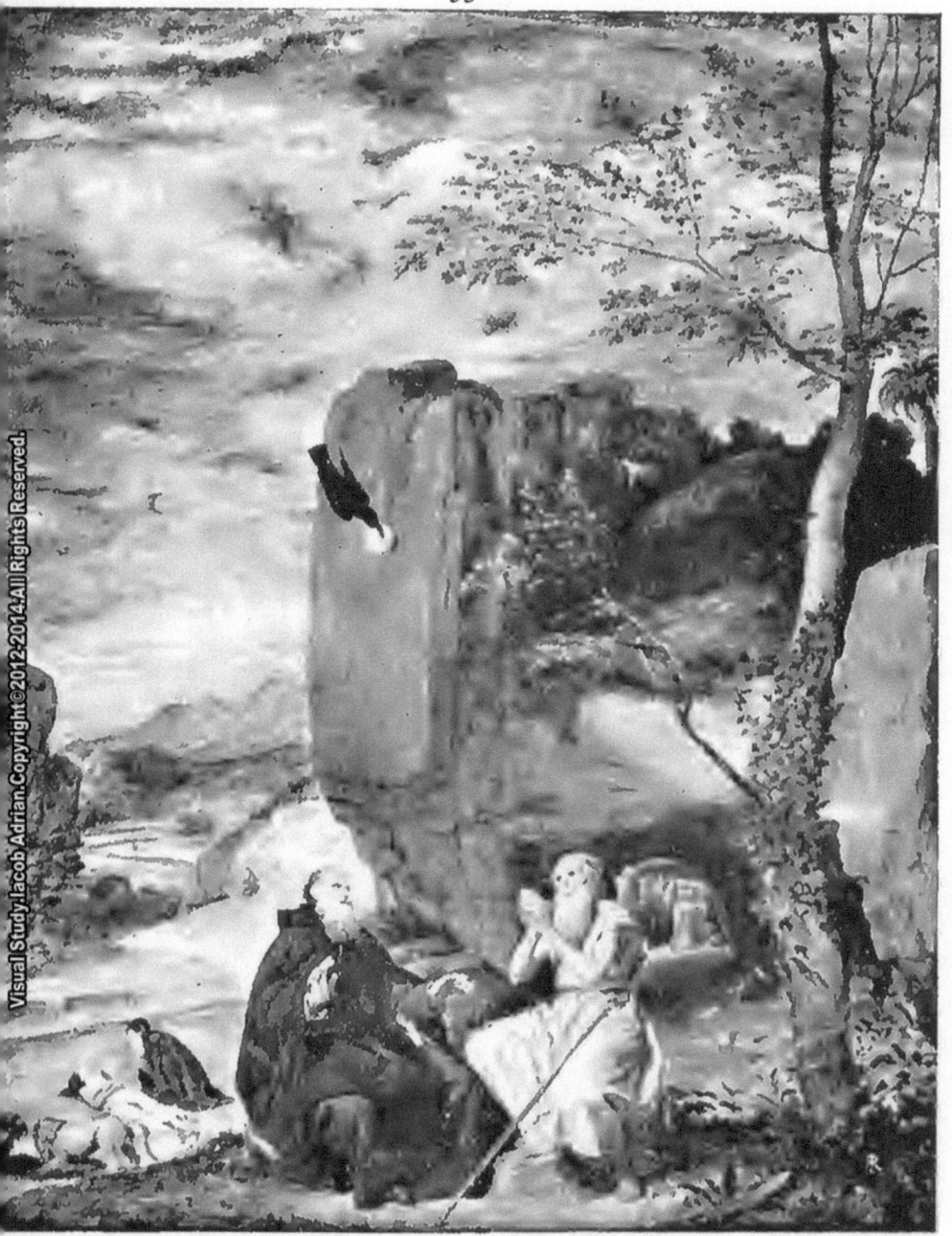

ST. ANTHONY AND ST. PAUL   SAINT ANTOINE ET SAINT PAUL
(Prado, Madrid)   *(Prado, Madrid)*
ST. ANTONIUS UND ST. PAUL
(Madrid, Prado)
D. Anderson, Photo.

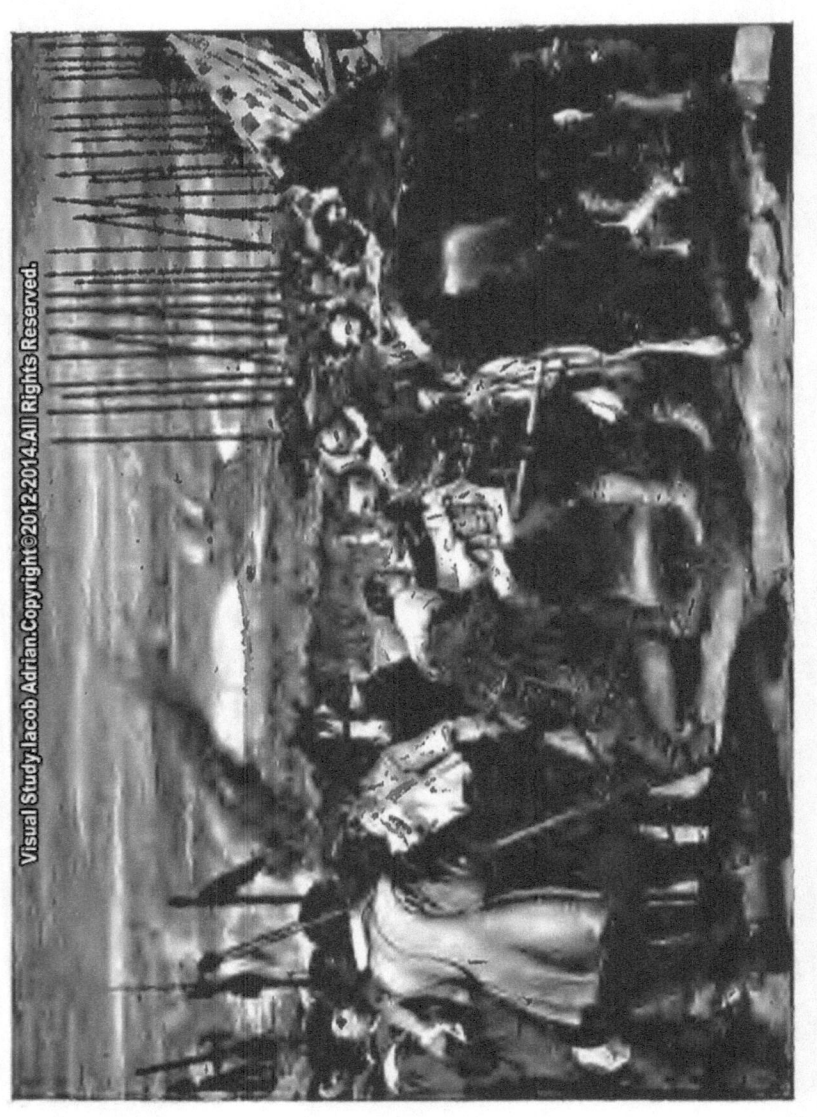

THE SURRENDER OF BREDA   LA REDDITION DE BREDA
(Prado, Madrid)   *(Prado, Madrid)*
DIE ERGEBUNG VON BREJA
(Madrid, Prado)
D. Anderson, photo.

55

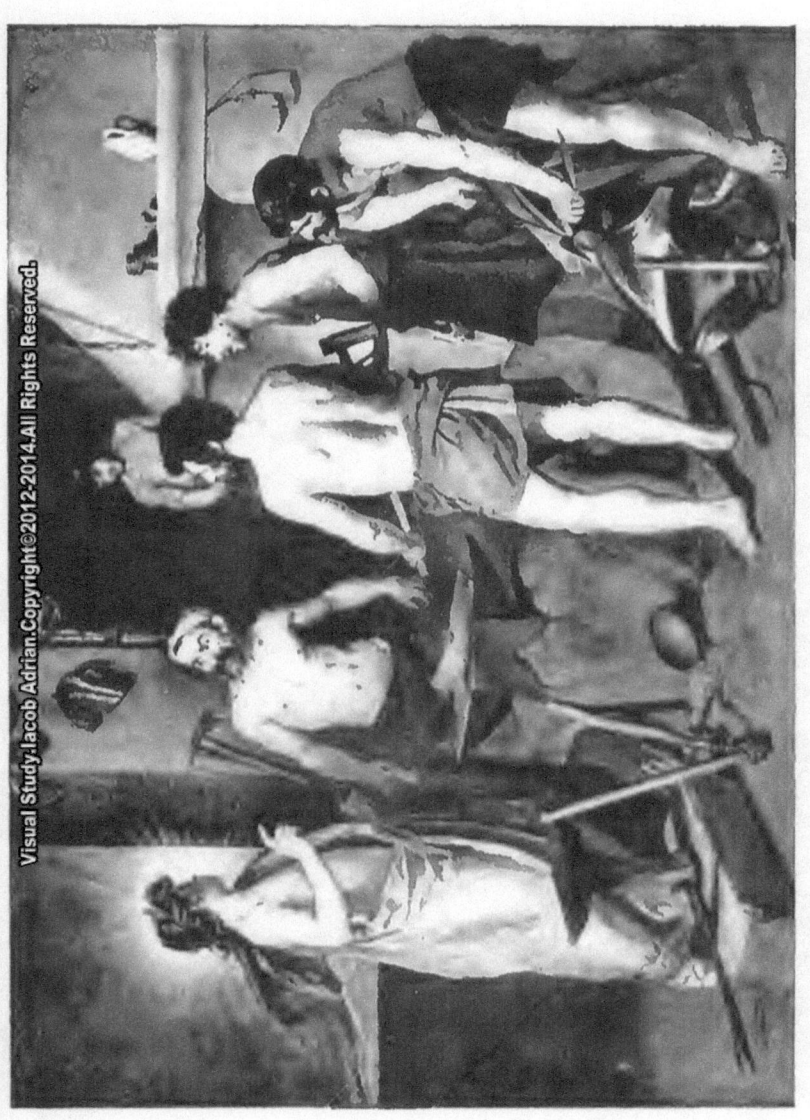

VULCAN'S FORGE
(*Prado, Madrid*)

VULKANS SCHMIEDE
(*Madrid, Prado*)
D. Anderson, Photo.

LA FORGE DE VULCAIN
(*Prado, Madrid*)

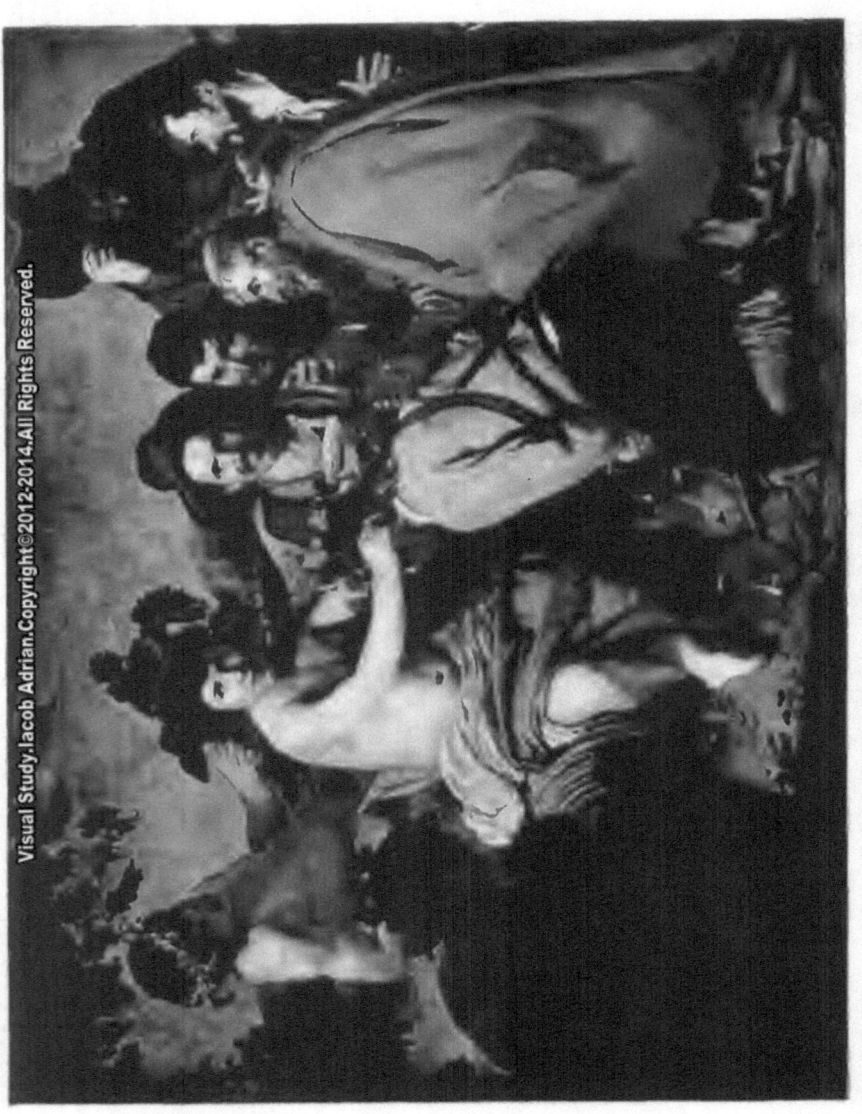

THE TOPERS
(*Prado, Madrid*)

DER TRIUMPH DES BACCHUS
(*Madrid, Prado*)
D. Anderson, Photo.

RÉUNION DE BUVEURS
(*Prado, Madrid*)

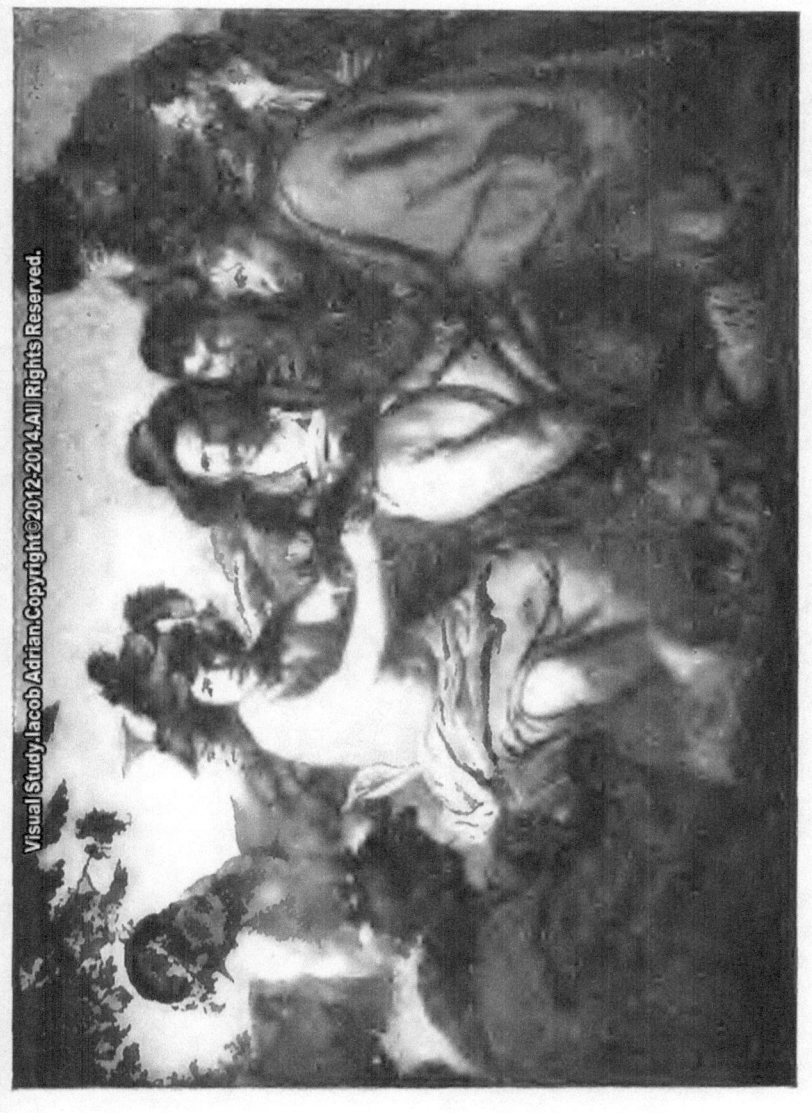

THE TOPERS
(*National Museum, Naples*)

DER TRIUMPH DES BACCHUS
(*Neapel, Nationalmuseum*)
F. Hanfstaengl, Photo.

RÉUNION DE BUVEURS
(*Musée national, Naples*)

58

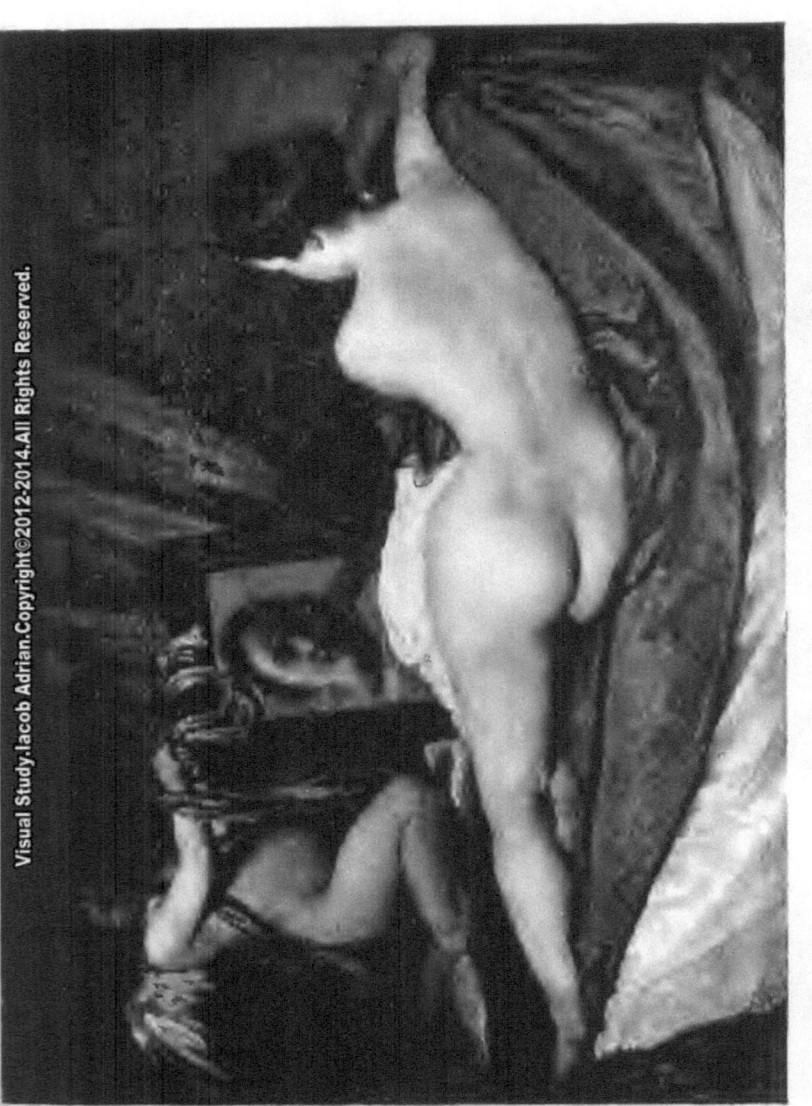

The " Rokeby " Venus
(*National Gallery, London*)

Ruhende Venus
(*London, Nationalgalerie*)
F. Hanfstaengl, Photo.

Vénus couchée
(*Galerie nationale, Londres*)

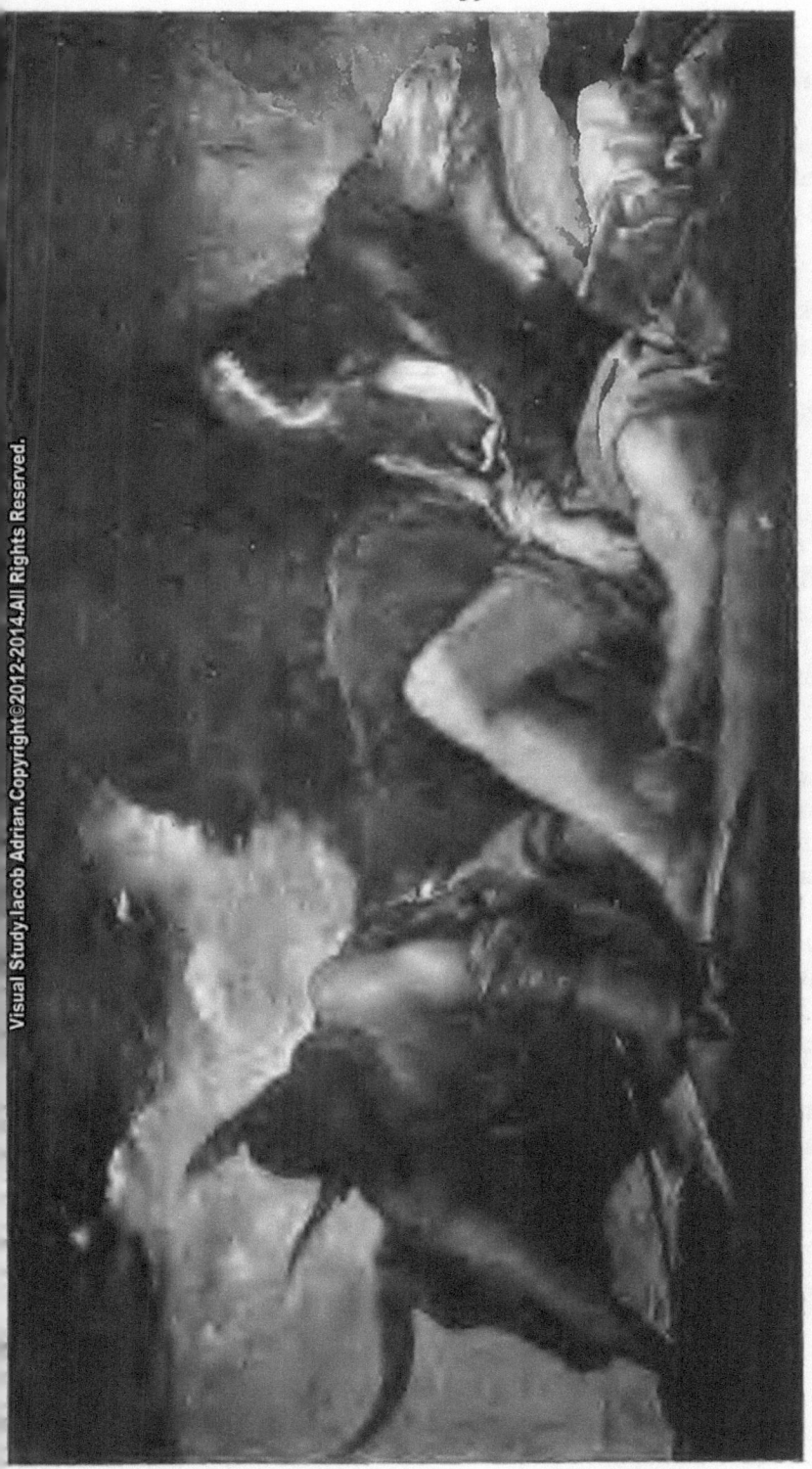

MERCURY AND ARGUS
(*Prado, Madrid*)

MERKUR UND ARGUS
(*Madrid, Prado*)
D. Anderson, Photo.

MERCURE ET ARGUS
(*Prado, Madrid*)

Bibliographic sources :

The masterpieces of Velazquez : sixty reproductions of photographs from
the original paintings, principally by F. Hanfstaengl, affording examples
of the different characteristics of the artist's work (1907)

Author:
Velázquez, Diego, 1599-1660;
Hanfstaengl, Franz, 1804-1877

Publisher: London ; Glasgow : Gowans & Gray, Ltd.

This documentary study use,
combined in various proportions,
elements from the following categories,
forms and subsets :
- fair use
- documentary
- documentary photography
- feature
- journalism
- arts journalism
- visual journalism
- photojournalism
- celebrity photography
in order to :
- employ material as the object of cultural critique ,
- quote to illustrate an argument or point ,
- use material in historical sequence,
providing independent opinion,
using photos, press articles, advertisements,
opinions of fans etc. ...